"Get ready to be empo[...] in every chapter face i[...] makes all things possible. Every woman needs this book!"
—Amy Seiffert, author of *Grace Looks Amazing on You,*
Starved, and *Your Name is Daughter*

"Remembering God's past faithfulness gives me such hope as we navigate the challenges of a broken world. Laura offers us the opportunity to reflect on the brave women of the Bible and how God was mighty in their lives. As we seek to develop courage and live as the daughters of God He has called us to be, we all need this message!"
—Rebecca George, author of *Do the Thing* and host of the
Radical Radiance podcast

"In *Brave Woman, Mighty God*, Laura L. Smith brings the stories of biblical women to life, from Miriam's songs to Abigail's courage to Huldah's esteemed faith. Smith connects these women's ancient journeys to our modern challenges, inspiring us to discover and use our gifts with the same emboldened faith of the biblical women who called out to God and, empowered by Him, rose up, reached out, and used their gifts. Laura has a gift of recognizing relevancy in biblical narratives and makes the Bible's story our story."
—Shena Ashcraft, Bible teacher and writer

"We so often hear about the men of the Word—what a gift to see light shed on the women. Laura is so exceptionally skilled at connecting our own everyday realities to the very real lived stories within the pages of Scripture. Her writing style is easy yet eloquent; she brings these biblical figures into your life not as unrelatable historical characters but as real women you can connect with—even see yourself in—and continue to learn from today. They are sisters and friends and mothers like us, and they are beautiful, broken, flawed, redeemed . . . like us.

Brave Woman, Mighty God is a beautiful reminder of the work God has started, which didn't end with them—and won't end with us. Beyond that, it's a reminder of how deeply God loves us and how intentionally He chooses us, in all our mess and whatever our circumstances, for our good and His glory."

—Erica Ligenza Gwynn, author, host of the *Thrive* podcast, and creator of cominguprosestheblog.com

Brave Woman, Mighty God

30 THINGS YOU **CAN** DO

LAURA L. SMITH

KREGEL
PUBLICATIONS

Brave Woman, Mighty God: 30 Things You Can Do
© 2025 by Laura L. Smith

Published by Kregel Publications, a division of Kregel Inc., 2450 Oak Industrial Dr. NE, Grand Rapids, MI 49505. www.kregel.com.

Laura L. Smith is represented by and *Brave Woman, Mighty God* is published in association with The Steve Laube Agency, LLC. www.stevelaube.com.

The persons and events portrayed in this book have been used with permission. To protect the privacy of these individuals, some names and identifying details have been changed.

All Scripture quotations, unless otherwise indicated, are taken from the Holy Bible, New International Version®, NIV®. Copyright © 1973, 1978, 1984, 2011 by Biblica, Inc.™ Used by permission of Zondervan. All rights reserved worldwide. www.zondervan.com. The "NIV" and "New International Version" are trademarks registered in the United States Patent and Trademark Office by Biblica, Inc.™

Scripture quotations marked MSG are taken from *The Message*, copyright © 1993, 2002, 2018 by Eugene H. Peterson. Used by permission of NavPress. All rights reserved. Represented by Tyndale House Publishers.

Scripture quotations marked NKJV are taken from the New King James Version®. Copyright © 1982 by Thomas Nelson. Used by permission. All rights reserved.

Scripture quotations marked NLT are taken from the *Holy Bible*, New Living Translation, copyright © 1996, 2004, 2015 by Tyndale House Foundation. Used by permission of Tyndale House Publishers, Carol Stream, Illinois 60188. All rights reserved.

Scripture quotations marked RSV are from Revised Standard Version of the Bible, copyright © 1946, 1952, and 1971 National Council of the Churches of Christ in the United States of America. Used by permission. All rights reserved worldwide.

Cataloging-in-Publication Data is available from the Library of Congress.

ISBN 978-0-8254-4892-8, print
ISBN 978-0-8254-6308-2, epub
ISBN 978-0-8254-6307-5, Kindle

Printed in the United States of America
25 26 27 28 29 30 31 32 33 34 / 5 4 3 2 1

*To Mom, Maddie, and Mallory—
the bravest women I know.*

Contents

Introduction

Growing up, I often felt powerless.

Powerless to say the right things or do the right things or be enough.

That sense of powerlessness seeped into my soul. I questioned my ability to excel, make a difference, change the way things were, step out, speak up, or have lasting, healthy relationships. This stemmed from some trauma at home. As a result, I doubted my worth, dreamed small, kept quiet, and did whatever I thought people expected of me, never questioning. Because the only thing I believed I had power over was my ability to do what I was told.

But as it turns out, I was empowered then and am still empowered now by the most powerful force in the universe—the mighty God who created it all. Empowered to live a full and abundant life. Empowered to do great things, brave things, hard things, important, life-changing, world-changing, kingdom-changing things, things for my good and God's glory.

You are too!

As Paul told the Ephesians (and us),

> I pray that the eyes of your heart may be enlightened in order that you may know the hope to which he has called you, the riches of his glorious inheritance in his holy people, and his incomparably great power for us who believe. That power is

the same as the mighty strength he exerted when he raised Christ from the dead and seated him at his right hand in the heavenly realms, far above all rule and authority, power and dominion, and every name that is invoked, not only in the present age but also in the one to come. (Ephesians 1:18–21)

Whoa! The same power that raised Christ from the dead is available to us. The power that is greater than any authority or ruler lives in you and me. I'm praying those verses over each reader of this book, that as you journey with me you'll discover and tap into this mighty power living in you and use it to do incredible, brave things.

The women in the Bible reveal to us ways our mighty God has always empowered women to be brave. When culture oppressed them, when people let them down, when fertility was a struggle, when life was dangerous, or when painful circumstances arose, God was there. Empowering woman after woman to bravely step into what He had for them. The women in the Bible who tapped into God's power, who understood the hope He calls us into, found purpose and satisfaction for their souls. These women saved lives, won battles, led God's people, protected the innocent, conquered evil, started over, spoke up. Their lives teach us so much about God's love for us, His plans for us, His promises to us, His protection over us. The power that these women possessed to do all these brave things? God offers this same mighty power to each and every one of us.

Growing up, I didn't give much thought to the women of the Bible. Sure, a few of these ladies showed up on felt boards and crafts in Sunday school. I knew some of their names—Eve, Sarah, Mary—but not much about them.

Apparently, things haven't changed. At least, not enough. But we're going to do something about that.

I was recently speaking to a group of high school girls about the women of the Bible and afterward a young lady came up to me and said, "Thank you so much. I'd never really thought about the women of the Bible before. I guess it's because they're not as important as the men, but . . ."

Gasp!

I didn't hear the rest of her sentence. *Never really thought . . . not as important.* She was missing out on so much. I could hear the professor from *The Lion, the Witch and the Wardrobe* saying in my mind, "Bless me, what *do* they teach them at these schools?"[1]

I looked the teen in her eyes and said, "The women were super important, just like the men. A woman in the Bible was the first person recorded leading worship. A woman in the Bible stopped a genocide. A woman in the Bible was the first person to share the gospel."

She got wide-eyed and excited—like I hope you do as you read this book. Like I did when I began truly learning about the women in the Bible.

The more I dove into their lives, their struggles, their triumphs, the more I wanted to learn. I grew to appreciate them, admire them, like them. The women of the Bible started to feel more like friends, fellow sojourners on this road of life, than just names in history.

The women in the Bible actually remind me of the various women who attend my Bible study—the one who's always early, the one who shows up halfway through, the one who is happily single, the one who wishes she was married, the one whose marriage looks like a dream, the one whose marriage is in shreds, the one who works a corporate job and shows up on her lunch break, the one who home-schools her kids and sets them up with workbooks in the adjoining room, the one who holds her worn leather Bible, and the one who holds her infant while we pray. The women of the Bible remind me of the quiet woman in the corner who always shows up but rarely speaks and of the woman who is chatting from the moment she walks in the door until she's back in her car an hour and a half later. The ones who cry, laugh, and can't wait until the coffee is brewed. I love them all, because they all show me a slice of God's kingdom and how He is alive and on the move. The more I get to know the ladies in my Bible study, the more I see the ways God sustains them, equips them, and gives them the courage they need to keep going and keep going well.

Women: God created each of us uniquely and remarkably, each of us exceptionally equipped to add to and grow God's kingdom, each of us made in His very image.

By knowing the women of the Bible, we women of today can better see how God is still here for us, still offering us the same power and purpose, the same courage, and the same satisfaction for our fractured souls.

Have you met or paid much attention to these ladies in the Bible? Are you curious to hear more about their stories? I'd like to introduce you to them. I'm praying that as you read, you notice how our mighty God equipped and empowered these women, how He made them brave, so you can better grasp how much power lives within you and how much you are capable of. With our mighty God on your side, the possibilities of what you can do are endless.

1

Call Out the Lies

Eve

As I rounded the corner, I heard a thud and glanced over to see that one nonfat caramel latte and two almond-milk mochas had tipped over in the passenger seat. I was able to stand them up quickly, but coffee had already escaped from the lids and left a small puddle on the leather seat of my husband's new car.

How could you be so foolish? How could you let this happen? Why are you so irresponsible? I heard a voice sneering inside my head.

Which really weren't questions, but accusations.

No one else was in the car. The voice wasn't what my husband would say to me or about me. The voice wasn't what I would tell any of my kids if they'd spilled. No, I'd say something like, "Oops. No big deal. Here's a napkin. Let's clean up the rest when we get home."

But the voice was one I'd heard before. Growing up, I'd heard similar phrases barked at me whenever I made a mess or a mistake. The person who spoke these words to me clearly wasn't in the car, but the soundtrack from my childhood replayed in my mind, making me doubt my value and worth, making me feel like a bad wife and mom all because the coffee tipped.

Did you notice the words? *Foolish. Irresponsible. You. You. You.*

None of which were true. It wasn't my fault the coffee spilled. It was an accident. I hadn't been foolish or irresponsible. The coffees were in a drink carrier that I had set upright on a flat surface. The cups had lids. They were presumably secure. I transport coffee like this all the time without spilling. And I certainly didn't *let* it happen. But the Enemy's aim is to make me feel like I'm not good enough. He'll do whatever it takes to pepper blame, shame, and guilt into my thought patterns. Which is the opposite of what God does.

I am not the first person that sneaky snake has tried this on. I'm betting he's tried it on you. And his tactics go way back to the very beginning.

God created Eve in His own image. He blessed her and her husband, Adam. He told them to fill the earth and subdue it. He gave them the power to rule over the earth. And then after declaring that everything else He had created was "good," God called man and woman "very good."

> So God created mankind in his own image,
>   in the image of God he created them;
>   male and female he created them. . . .
>
> Then God said [to them], "I give you every seed-bearing plant on the face of the whole earth and every tree that has fruit with seed in it. They will be yours for food. And to all the beasts of the earth and all the birds in the sky and all the creatures that move along the ground—everything that has the breath of life in it—I give every green plant for food." And it was so. (Genesis 1:27, 29–30)

Adam and Eve were living in the actual garden of Eden—paradise. What a life! But then the Serpent found Eve one day and slithered in with an accusation meant to sound like a question, emphasizing the word *you*.

"Did God really say, 'You must not eat from any tree in the garden'?" (Genesis 3:1).

God didn't say anything like that. But the Enemy was crafty. He twisted words to make them confusing. God had told Adam and Eve they could eat *any* fruit that had seeds (meaning it could create more fruit). I'm picturing a peach—remarkably fuzzy yet edible. How if you slice into it, thick nectar drips out that tastes like summer. I'm picturing cherry trees, orange trees, plum trees—all kinds of trees loaded with bright, sweet, ripe fruit packed with nutrients, all planted in the same magnificent garden.

God never said, "You must not eat from any tree."

But the seed of doubt was planted in Eve's mind. She tried to correct Satan: "Wait. God said we can eat fruit from the trees, but . . ." As she considered the question, she remembered there was one thing God wouldn't let her do. Maybe she wondered for the very first time, *Why won't He?* Eve finished her response to the Serpent. "God did say, 'You must not eat fruit from the tree that is in the middle of the garden, and you must not touch it, or you will die'" (verses 2–3).

And then that Serpent had Eve where he wanted her. He tricked her into saying God wouldn't let her do something—as if God were restricting her, limiting her, keeping her from something good. The Enemy inserted doubt and twisted it around a bit. *Why would God do that? Why, if God loved you, Eve, would He not let you have everything?* But the truth was that God loved Eve so much He gave her and Adam free rein of the garden. There was only one fruit they couldn't have, out of *all* the fruit they could, and it was only to protect them, not deny them. Kind of like how I won't let my daughter with a nut allergy eat a brownie with walnuts sprinkled on top. I'm not denying her. I'm protecting her.

Satan has been inserting doubt into our minds and twisting it around ever since. *Oh, you didn't get the scholarship, promotion, engagement ring, deal, bid, shout-out, invitation, better office, prize, bigger portion, first choice? Perhaps it's because you're not good enough, not liked as much, don't have what it takes,* the Enemy whispers.

But God clearly states we are loved, we are His daughters, part of a royal priesthood, mighty warriors, and made in His image. Which means whatever we do or do not win, earn, or achieve, we are still loved. God still considers us royalty. God still empowers us with His might. We can be brave because He is on our side. And we still (and always will) reflect the very image of the living God. So all that mumbo jumbo about "not enough" from the Enemy? It's ridiculous.

But the Enemy is relentless. He gets us alone and starts in with the lies. Big ones. Small ones. Silly ones. Irrelevant ones. Lies that sting like salt in a wound. They sound like questions, but they're actually accusations. *Why didn't you try harder? What makes you think you're qualified? Do you think anyone really wants to hear/see/try/taste that thing you made, that idea you have? Remember how your last relationship/job/attempt worked out? What makes you think it will be better this time? Why didn't you work out more, study longer, be more careful, pipe down, speak out, grow out your bangs?*

The Enemy is a liar. But the Bible is pure truth. It reminds us: There is no condemnation in Christ Jesus (Romans 8:1).

None.

Jesus loves you. Always. Forever. Right here. Right now.

The Enemy wants you to lose sight of that.

Don't listen to him.

Whose voice are you listening to today?

God's?

Or the thief's, who comes to steal, kill, and destroy (John 10:10)? The Enemy is lurking, trying to get God's people alone and confuse them about who they are in Christ. Eve had been living her best life, eating delicious fresh fruit daily with the perfect man for her, and then the Serpent came in with his smoke screen of finger-pointing accusations. Next thing you know, Eve was hiding in the bushes, ashamed. How did she go from absolute freedom to cowering behind branches?

She listened to the wrong voice.

Instead of dismissing his lies, she believed the Enemy's accusation that God was keeping something from her.

We, like Eve, get to choose who we listen to. But we have something she didn't. We have Eve's story. And God made sure her story was in the Bible for us to learn from. We know how that snake manipulated Eve into listening to him instead of God. We can learn from her mistake and tell that slippery Serpent that he's a liar and we're not going to listen to his trash talk anymore.

In the car with the spilled coffee, I had to talk myself out of a spiral of negative self-talk and challenge the Enemy. I did it out loud.

"What?" I challenged the Enemy. "I wasn't being foolish or irresponsible. I didn't *let* the coffee spill. Those thoughts, statements, whatever, aren't true. And they have no business in this car or in my head. They are lies."

It felt good to call out the lies. And I felt so much peace.

It takes effort and intentionality to overcome the lies of the Enemy—they're so slippery and sneaky and constant. But God is mighty and empowers us to question the accusations and bravely dismantle the lies. This is what it looks like to follow Paul's instructions to the Corinthians: "We take captive every thought to make it obedient to Christ" (2 Corinthians 10:5). We call out the lie for what it is. And we take it down.

> God is mighty and empowers us to question the accusations and bravely dismantle the lies.

At age sixteen or twenty-six, I would have been mortified by the spill. *How could I let such a thing happen?* My shame would have felt like walking through the dense, gray smog of a smoke bomb, making me feel sick, disoriented, cloudy, muddled, and worthless. And it would have led me to be dishonest about the whole thing. I would have been terrified to tell anyone. I would have sneaked into the house, crept back out with cleaning supplies, and tried to erase any evidence of the spill. I would have kept my mouth shut, allowing the shame to fester where it was trapped inside.

But that day? I carried the coffees inside, took a long sip of my rich mocha, set all the cups on our red kitchen table, grabbed paper towels and some lavender-scented cleaning spray, cleaned up the small spill in the car, came back inside, carried my hubby's coffee to him in his home office, and told him the whole story.

"You know I'd never say that to you, don't you?" Brett said as he looked me in the eyes.

"Yup. I do. And thank you for loving me like that."

"It's just a car. And just a spill. Thank you for getting me coffee." Brett held his paper cup up in a toast.

His voice sounded a lot more like God's, and like truth, and like the voice I want to listen to.

How did I get to this place of recognizing lies and calling them out?

It took a while. And I still don't always get it right.

But the more time I spend with God, talk to Jesus, and read my Bible, the more God teaches me how to distinguish lies from truth, God's voice from the Enemy's. This will work for you too.

You might not get worked up about spilling something. Maybe you worry about what people think of your performance, your home, your outfit, your kids' behavior, or the words you speak. Those are important things to value, but let's do this right.

Eve may be famous for eating the forbidden fruit. But God didn't give up on her then, or ever. After the whole hiding-in-the-bushes incident, God sought Eve out, clothed her, blessed her, and protected her. God never stopped loving her, and that enabled Eve to bravely move forward from that devastating day with the Serpent to become the mother of all mankind, teaching her children to worship God. Our mighty God loves you and me with that same perfect love.

Let's listen to God's loving voice. Make it the loudest one in our heads. He frees us from shame and invites us into an abundant life. Stand up. Lift your head. Take a step forward. Oh, and yeah, tell the Enemy he's a liar.

Call Out the Lies

So God created mankind in his own image,
in the image of God he created them;
male and female he created them. . . .

God saw all that he had made, and it was very good. (Genesis 1:27, 31)

- What are you focusing on today? The smoke screen the Enemy has put before you? Or the truth of who God created you to be?
- What are some current thoughts you have about yourself?
- Eve learned the hard way that the Serpent likes to whisper lies and accusations. Let's combat the lies that bombard us by speaking out loud the statements below that are backed by Bible verses. If any of the thoughts in the previous question were negative, write one of these verses over it. Maybe make one of these verses your new screen saver or write it on a note card and stick it to your mirror.

  I am made in the image of God (Genesis 1:27).

  I am Christ's prized possession (1 Peter 2:9).

  I am Christ's masterpiece (Ephesians 2:10).

  God has plans to prosper me (Jeremiah 29:11).

  God promises to never leave me (Hebrews 13:5).

2

Hold Out for Happily-Ever-After

Sarah

I love a good princess story—from watching Cinderella swirl around in her blue dress when I was a little girl, to singing the songs from *The Little Mermaid* and *Tangled* with my daughters, I love happily-ever-afters. In all these movies, it seems like the struggling young women become princesses in an instant. We sit for an hour and a half with our buttery popcorn and fluffy fleece blankets and watch them go from rejected to wearing tiaras, all before bedtime.

But real life doesn't play out like that.

In fact, even in these movies, if we really dug deep, most of the heroines have handfuls of hardships before finding their happiness. For years and years Cinderella is a servant for her stepmother and stepsisters before she gets bibbidi-bobbidi-booed into a ball gown and glass slippers. Ariel has been longing to be part of the humans' world for ages. And Rapunzel is gaslighted most of her life and has a near-death experience, for goodness' sake.

In the Bible, a woman named Sarai struggled for decades before finding her fairy-tale ending. God promised Sarai and her husband,

Abram, as many kids, grandkids, great-grands, and so on as stars in the sky (Genesis 15:5). Sarai's culture wasn't concerned about a woman's career, community service, or contributions; it measured a woman's value on one thing—her ability to have children, specifically boys, to add to the family line. So that promise of a multitude of descendants was her ultimate happily-ever-after. But Sarai had fertility issues.

When her husband, Abram, was seventy-five, God told him:

> Go from your country, your people and your father's household to the land I will show you.
>
> I will make you into a great nation,
>   and I will bless you;
> I will make your name great,
>   and you will be a blessing.
> I will bless those who bless you,
>   and whoever curses you I will curse;
> and all peoples on earth
>   will be blessed through you.
>
> (Genesis 12:1–3)

When God speaks like this, you do it. So, at around age sixty-five, Sarai went with her husband away from their home, her friends and community, her favorite well to fetch fresh water from, and the peaceful place to take walks she'd discovered. Sarai obediently went with Abram, followed God's instructions, and trusted God's promise of future blessings. But this wasn't the part where singing mice and birds started sewing Sarai a maternity gown. No, this was the plot twist where there was a famine, and Sarai and Abram had to travel farther than planned to find food. They arrived in Egypt, and Abram freaked out because he was afraid the pharaoh would kill him to try to take his gorgeous wife. To protect himself, Abram told Pharaoh that Sarai was his sister. Oh yeah, and Abram told Sarai to go along with the charade.

This was not God's plotline; this was one Abram wrote for himself. But God made a promise. And He always keeps His promises. So even though Abram made a mess of things, God got things back on track by getting Pharaoh to send Sarai and Abram out of town—and fast.

By the time Sarai was seventy-six, she'd lost faith in God's promise. It had been over ten years since God sent them. Blessings? Descendants? She sure didn't see them.

When I got pregnant with our fourth child, I was told I was of "advanced maternal age." In her mid-seventies, Sarai way exceeded that. She gave up hope, figured she'd waited enough, and took things into her own hands. Sarai sent her servant, Hagar, to sleep with Abram, hoping Hagar would get pregnant and provide Abram with an heir. Desperate people do desperate things.

It "worked." Hagar got pregnant and had a son, someone to carry on Abram's name. But, not surprisingly, it was an ugly disaster of jealousy, pain, and shame for both women. This had never been God's plan.

Despite Sarai doubting God and thinking she could handle this better than Him, when Sarai was eighty-nine, God said to Abram (whom He had just renamed Abraham), "As for Sarai your wife, you are no longer to call her Sarai; her name will be Sarah. I will bless her and will surely give you a son by her. I will bless her so that she will be the mother of nations; kings of peoples will come from her" (Genesis 17:15–16).

Sarah. It means "princess."[1]

A year later, at age ninety, Sarah gave birth to a son and named him Isaac. You'll find him on Jesus's family tree (Luke 3:34; Matthew 1:2). Even though her family line would face major struggles, as all families do, Sarah found her happily-ever-after.

For the record, *Sarai* also meant "princess."[2] That had always been God's plan for her. It just took a while for Sarai to learn to trust God in this plan, to stop trying to do things by herself, to stop disregarding God's promises as ridiculous. Sarah actually laughed out loud one of the times God promised she'd have a son (Genesis 18:12). It took time and mistakes before Sarah leaned into God's promises and believed that what He said about her was true.

How are you doing with this? With trusting what God says about you even when the world tells you that you don't measure up? With patiently waiting for God to make good on His promises even if it's taking longer than you hoped? Way longer.

Are you taking things into your own hands like the Little Mermaid trading her voice for legs or Sarah forcing her servant to have sex with her husband in hopes of getting a son? Trying to out-plan God, because what if you just tried *this*? Are you laughing off God's promises because they seem far-fetched? God's plans do sound crazy sometimes, but He's God. He can do anything.

On any given day I could be doing both splendidly and horribly in all these areas. But thankfully, God is patient with us, He loves us, and He keeps His promises.

> God's plans do sound crazy sometimes,
> but He's God. He can do anything.

Before Sarah was born, God knew He would choose her to be the wife of Abraham, that kings would come from her. In God's eyes, she was always a princess, but she struggled to see it. Sarai, the one who had been thrown into Pharaoh's harem by her own husband, and who had lost hope and orchestrated for her husband to sleep with another woman. God renamed her a princess, showing Sarah this wasn't just a name her parents gave her, but the name *He* gave her. This renaming by God was significant. It gave Sarah newfound strength and bravery to step into her new role as the mother of the entire Hebrew nation, even earning her a mention in the famous Hall of Faith (Hebrews 11:11). The name of Sarah gave her that new chance that Cinderella, Ariel, and Rapunzel all craved, one that I believe God has put a desire for in *all* our hearts—a longing for something more fulfilling and beautiful than what we've known before. God wants us to seek Him, just like the fairy-tale princesses seek someone who will see and love them for their true selves. God places that longing inside of us because He's the one who can fulfill it.

Our Prince is more amazing than any Disney artist could create. We have a Prince who rides a mighty white steed, swoops in, picks us up, and sees and loves us for exactly who we are. He believes we are valuable and lovable and wants to live with us happily ever after. His name is Jesus.

> I saw heaven standing open and there before me was a white horse, whose rider is called Faithful and True. With justice he judges and wages war. His eyes are like blazing fire, and on his head are many crowns. He has a name written on him that no one knows but he himself. He is dressed in a robe dipped in blood, and his name is the Word of God. (Revelation 19:11–13)

Wherever you are in your story, remember that God is the author and perfecter of your faith (Hebrews 12:2). As the author of your story, He's written you the happiest of endings.

Sure, it won't all be skipping through wildflowers along the way.

We might get locked in a closet or tricked by someone who tries to con us out of our birthright. We might choose the wrong path through the forest, trust the wrong person, get distracted, try to do things our own way, lose hope, doubt, or eat a poison apple. But Jesus is Faithful and True, and He's the one who gets to write the ending. He'll empower you to do the things He promises. So, no matter what you've done, where you've gotten off track, how strong or weak your faith is today, God calls you His daughter, part of His royal family, and He longs to live happily ever after throughout eternity with you.

Hold Out for Happily-Ever-After

> I saw heaven standing open and there before me was a white horse, whose rider is called Faithful and True. (Revelation 19:11)

- Is there something you feel God has promised that seems to be taking a long time? Talk or journal to Him about it. He is your loving Father and wants to hear it all. Tell God your hopes and dreams and how your heart feels in the midst of the disappointment or waiting.
- Ask God to bring Sarah's story to mind in the coming days and weeks, using it to remind you that He'll be just as faithful to you as He was to Sarah (even when it felt like it was taking forever).
- Ask Jesus to give you hope and endurance to stand strong as you wait for His timing.

3

Call for Help

Hagar

This chapter will discuss the topic of sexual assault.
Please take care when reading.

I'd been at college only a couple of weeks when I agreed to be set up for a casual "dorm date party" with a tall, handsome athlete. He was funny and liked the same music I did. We talked for hours, and at the end of the evening he quickly kissed me good night. I liked him.

We flirted back and forth a bit in the dining hall, but to my disappointment nothing came of it. During my sophomore year he was in one of my classes. The flirting and kissing resumed briefly. I knew he wasn't good for me. He clearly didn't want to date, just flirt and make out from time to time. But he was cute. And I was in a season of making bad decisions.

The summer between my junior and senior years, I was on campus for a few weeks for an introduction to my study-abroad program. Guess who was taking summer school classes? I was out with friends and ran into the guy. He walked me back to my apartment and stepped inside. We started kissing. Then he pushed me to the floor.

He was over six feet tall and strong—a college athlete. My arms were the diameter of pencils. Did I mention I was living alone? My roommates had all gone home for the summer. I tried to push him off me, but it was useless. There was no one there to help. I tried to shrink into the scratchy beige carpet, as far away from him as I could get. But he was still on top of me. I told him to stop, to get off.

No one except the guy could hear my muffled pleas.

I squirmed and shoved and screamed.

After a few frightening moments of fearing the worst, miraculously he stood and left.

I rushed to the door, locked it behind him, and collapsed into a terrified heap. Adrenaline rushed through my veins. My heart pounded inside my chest like a bass drum, shaking me to my core. For a long time, I couldn't move, frozen on the carpet.

Although I'd felt all alone, there was Someone with me, inside the walls of my apartment, who heard my desperate cries. God saw me. He heard me. And He saved me.

Had I done all the right things?

No.

Had I been actively seeking God's will for my life?

Clearly not.

I was intentionally kissing a guy I wasn't dating and who I knew was bad news. I blamed myself. But the blame wasn't mine to shoulder. For the kissing, yes. For the shove to the floor, 100 percent no. I saw myself as a girl who'd made a mistake and gotten herself into this mess. God saw me as His daughter. His beautiful creation. The one He intentionally knit together stitch by stitch while I was still in my mother's womb (Psalm 139:13). If you've been in a similar situation or if your situation was worse, possibly even much worse, God saw you then and sees you now as His beautiful creation and daughter too.

God never loses sight of us or of who He created us to be, even when we lose sight of ourselves.

Do you remember Hagar from the previous chapter? Sarai's Egyptian slave? The one Sarai gave to her husband as a bonus wife—solely to have sex with Abram in hopes she'd get pregnant and give him kids. Hagar's situation was horrific. But like me, like you, she was not forgotten by God.

As an Egyptian, Hagar would have worshiped the Egyptian gods—the sun god, the earth god, the motherhood goddess, the war goddess, and many others. She grew up praying to statues. Hagar most likely witnessed Sarai and Abram praying to God, but they treated her like dirt. Why would she want to believe what they believed?

God never loses sight of us or of who He created us to be, even when we lose sight of ourselves.

The Bible tells us in Genesis 16:4 that once pregnant, Hagar despised Sarai. That didn't mean Hagar just held a grudge. The original Hebrew is translated "to curse" or "be despicable toward," so Hagar was downright mean to her mistress. Now, Hagar was a slave who was forced to have sex with a married man, so she had every right to be angry. But Hagar's rage sent Sarai seething, even though Sarai had arranged the whole "why don't you get pregnant with my husband's child" thing. Sarai lashed back and "afflicted" Hagar.

In that time women had little value, and slaves were even lower on the totem pole. So a female slave? She barely had any voice. After the brawl, Hagar fled to the wilderness, which was dangerous and terrifying. She was all alone and could have been attacked by wild animals or starved to death. Who would even know? If Hagar were discovered by travelers, she could have been raped, abused, or murdered. No one would hear her cries for help. And if they did, they might not have cared.

But then the most remarkable thing happened. God sent an angel to help this woman who didn't even worship Him, the woman with negligible worth to her household and culture, and the woman who had just broken the law by running away from her master. You see, the world saw Hagar as almost worthless. She might have seen herself that way too. But God? He created Hagar. He loved her. And God never loses sight of His children.

The angel of the Lord found Hagar beside a spring of water in the wilderness, along the road to Shur. The angel said to her, "Hagar, Sarai's servant, where have you come from, and where are you going?"

"I'm running away from my mistress, Sarai," she replied.

The angel of the Lord said to her, "Return to your mistress, and submit to her authority." Then he added, "I will give you more descendants than you can count."

And the angel also said, "You are now pregnant and will give birth to a son. You are to name him Ishmael (which means 'God hears'), for the Lord has heard your cry of distress." (Genesis 16:7–11 NLT)

The Lord has heard your cry of distress.

Wherever you are. Whatever you're in the middle of today, right now. No matter what you did or didn't do to get there. No matter if you landed there as a result of your own mistakes or what someone else did or circumstances or culture. No matter where you are in your relationship with God. Even if you think no one can hear you. Even if you think no one will answer if you call for help. God. Hears. You.

He'll answer your calls. He wants to offer you better. You can call out to Him for help.

God rescued Hagar in the wilderness. God saw her. Called her by name. Blessed her. Bearing kids was the endgame for women at that time, and God promised Hagar more descendants than she could count. I can't imagine having to head back to Abram and Sarai's tents. But our mighty God gave Hagar the strength and courage she needed. He also gave her a plan to move forward.

Based on the tracking information on our phones, I can "see" my kids. But I can't *actually* see them. I might know one of my daughters is at her part-time job at the local ice cream shop, but I can't tell if she's relaxed or stressed or if any of her friends stopped by to say hi. I can see that one of my kids is at practice, but is he having fun or feeling the pressure of the intimidating coach? I can tell if my kids are at school, but did they eat their lunch? How did they do on that test they were worried about? Did they share the awesome thing they did yesterday with any of their pals?

I can know my kids' locations without knowing how they're doing. But God *sees us* sees us. And not just in the generic "Oh look, Laura's typing on her laptop right now" way, but in the "truly knowing our thoughts"—our worries, fears, hopes, and dreams—kind of way. God sees you specifically.

Let that sink in for a moment. God sees you, all of you, and loves you no matter what. Mind-blowing, right?

Overwhelmed by this astonishing truth, Hagar declared, "You are the God who sees me" and "I have now seen the One who sees me" (Genesis 16:13).

Hagar was the first person in Scripture to name God. Her encounter with Him changed her and made her braver than she'd ever been. Hagar named God how she knew Him—the God who saw her. This same God sees you and is ready to rescue you when you call for help.

Hagar's life didn't become all sunshine and roses because she learned how much God loved her. God told Hagar to go back to Sarai, who had been mean with a capital *M*, and submit to her mistress. Not exactly a dream come true. But the alternative was to die a horrible death in the wilderness, alone and frightened. God knew going back would provide safety, food, and the influential family name of Abram for Hagar and the son growing inside her. God is always looking out for us. He hears our cries. He sees us and answers our calls for help.

God saw me struggling on my apartment floor that summer night. He heard my desperate cries and helped me. In retrospect, I believe that God also saw the college guy I referenced, that God whispered to him to stop so he wouldn't end up doing something he'd forever regret. Because he chose to leave, we were both saved in that moment. But even if he would have chosen differently, I know God still would have heard and seen me. God still would have comforted me and helped me heal from that terrible act.

Sadly, not all potential perpetrators choose to listen to God. We live in a broken world. Sexual assault is a devastating reality that harms one out of every five women in the United States.[1] God hears these victims' cries. If this is you or someone you love, God sees you in your pain. He longs to help you heal from the trauma of being violated. God is right beside you, loving you, weeping with you, and ready to help you move forward.[2]

God knows whatever you're in the midst of—physical pain, depression, loss, or an empty bank account. He sees you in your struggles, hears you when you cry. No matter if you're turning to Jesus for help or trying to do it all by yourself or even if you're on your worst behavior. That June evening in college I felt helpless, like no one knew where I was. I'm guessing Hagar felt the same while alone in the wilderness. But there is nowhere where we are too far out of sight for God or too far out of His earshot. Nowhere.

> For I am convinced that neither death nor life, neither angels nor demons, neither the present nor the future, nor any powers, neither height nor depth, nor anything else in all creation, will be able to separate us from the love of God that is in Christ Jesus our Lord. (Romans 8:38–39)

Call for Help

You are the God who sees me. (Genesis 16:13)

- Is there some part of your life where you feel alone? Like nobody hears or sees you? God is the God who sees you. Ask Him to make Himself known to you. Ask Him to help you see and feel that He is right beside you.
- Write this out: *Nothing can separate me from the love of Jesus.* Write it again and again until it sinks in.
- Have you called out to God like Hagar did? If not, try now. Even if you have, now's a great time to call out to Him again. You could:

  Close your eyes and hold out your hands, palms up.

Ask God to help you feel His presence.

Tell Him the thing you think no one hears. Ask for His help.

End by saying out loud, "Nothing can separate me from the love of Jesus. Amen."

4

Walk Through the Door

Rebekah

The on-campus house was packed with college kids praising Jesus. This wasn't some national ministry or publicized event or a Christian college's programming but an informal worship gathering at a public university. The worship leader gently played a melody on his keyboard while a man in his late twenties testified how God had called him and his wife to stay in this college town after they graduated. As the man shared his story, I felt God reminding me of when He told me and my husband to move back to this same college town when I was pregnant with our second child. I smiled to God, thanking Him for sending us here all those years ago.

We love our life in this tiny town covered in brick and ivy and over the years have seen the countless reasons why God asked us to leave our lives in suburban Atlanta to move here. My husband has his dream job as a professor at our alma mater. We've met so many incredible people. We raised our four kids in this wonderful town that, although small in population, offers a large variety of speakers, performances, cultural and sporting events, and experiences. But in this precise moment, in a room predominantly full of college students who had gathered to worship Jesus, I realized yet another reason why God had called us here. Our son Max was the one playing keys, leading the gathering. In this place and time, it was our son's voice being used to grow the kingdom. And it was Max who was the baby in my womb when God told us to move here. God knew *then* that He would use Max *now* to lead this grassroots student movement to love and honor Jesus *if* we walked through the door God opened for us over two decades ago.

What if we'd said no?

Would this gathering even be taking place?

Would some of these college students even know Jesus?

Would Max have led a student group to love Jesus in Atlanta?

Would God have found someone else to point these Gen-Zers to Jesus if we'd never come?

I'll never know. But I see what God did with our yes. I see how God planned for this moment now twenty-two years ago. When God says He has plans for us in Jeremiah 29:11, He isn't kidding! How intricate and personal is our God if He could plan this moment over two decades ago?

What door is God nudging you to walk through today?

What are all the excuses in your head for why it doesn't make sense?

What are all the what-if questions running through your brain? *What if I go there and I have to say goodbye to that person? What if it takes time away from this responsibility or risks jeopardizing the situation? What if it's too expensive or lets my family down?*

Maybe those things will be a problem. But maybe not. You can pray about the issues you're worried about. You can trust Jesus to take care of the details. He's pretty powerful, you know. Not to mention this truth: If God calls us to something, there is reason and purpose, and His perspective of the big picture is so much grander than ours. Maybe instead of worrying about what might happen, we could instead dream of how God might equip us, use us, empower us to do mighty things in His name for our good and His glory. What if we imagine Him opening new doors for us that lead to grand places?

I wonder what doubts were in Rebekah's brain when God opened a door for her.

Rebekah was living in her hometown of Haran with her family when a stranger approached her at the public well and asked for a drink. She gave the man a drink from her jug, which was simply good manners. But then Rebekah went above and beyond. She saw the man had ten camels and that he was clearly a traveler. She offered to get water for all his camels, which would have been about 250 gallons of water. Would you volunteer to lug 250 gallons of water over to a stranger's smelly animals? *Um, not it.*

> If God calls us to something, there is reason and purpose, and His perspective of the big picture is so much grander than ours.

Then the story gets even more interesting. The stranger whipped out some gold jewelry, gave it to Rebekah, asked who her family was and if they would put him up for the night. In Rebekah's culture, asking for a room was normal. There weren't Hyatts, Hiltons, or Holiday Inns, so locals often opened their homes to travelers.

Back at Rebekah's house, the stranger announced that he worked for her wealthy out-of-town uncle, Abraham. The stranger also shared that he was on a mission to find a wife for Abraham's son, Isaac, a.k.a. Rebekah's cousin. The traveler went on to explain how he'd prayed ahead of time for God to reveal to him the woman who should be Isaac's bride and that God specifically answered his prayers through the actions, words, and timing of his encounter with Rebekah.

Convinced this was Rebekah's destiny, her dad and brother agreed for the man to take Rebekah with him so she could marry Isaac, but when the stranger insisted on taking her the next morning, her family wasn't so sure.

Then [Rebekah's mom and brother] said, "Let's call the young woman and ask her about it." So they called Rebekah and asked her, "Will you go with this man?"

"I will go," she said.

So they sent their sister Rebekah on her way, along with her nurse and Abraham's servant and his men. (Genesis 24:57–59)

Bear with me for a tad more cultural context. A woman's goal in life in Haran was to marry a man who could provide for her. I know, I know. I'm grateful that's not our present reality, but for Rebekah it was. So an offer to marry a rich man who was a trusted relative was like getting accepted to Harvard in terms of securing her future. Still, it wasn't that simple. Rebekah would have to leave everything she knew—her family, her home, her friends, the brick walls that protected her city, the dishes, vases, and containers in her home decorated with geometric designs and animals that her town was known for. She'd have to leave all this familiarity to marry a man she'd never met, the son of an uncle she'd never met. To live in a place she'd never seen, among unfamiliar household items. Rebekah had just met the man she would be traveling with, and the route to her future husband was between four hundred and six hundred miles. By camel.

What questions whirled through her head? *Is this man legit? Does he really work for Abraham? What's Isaac like? I know absolutely nothing about him. Will he be kind to me? Is he cute? Is he smart? Is he funny? Who will help my mom run the household if I leave? How will I survive weeks of travel? Who will I talk to? Won't that be exhausting? Lonely? Won't I get bored?*

But somehow amid all the uncertainty, Rebekah decided to walk through the door God opened for her and said three words that changed history: "I will go" (verse 58).

I wonder what nudges God gave her leading up to that yes. Did God urge Rebekah's mom to ask Rebekah to go to the well at the exact time the stranger arrived? Did God prompt Rebekah to offer the stranger water for his camels, knowing that was part of the man's prayer? Did God whisper in Rebekah's ear to tell the man, "We have plenty of straw and fodder, as well as room for you to spend the night" (verse 25)?

What if she had said no? What if Rebekah had dawdled and gone to the well an hour later? What if she was in a rush to go to the well, and even though God told her it would be a good idea to wait, she went early? What if she agreed to give the man some water but was eager to get moving, so she did her cultural obligation and scooted out of there? What if Rebekah had hesitated and said, "I'm not sure if we have room and food for all those camels. Let me check with my dad first"? What if when her mom and brother asked, "Will you go?" she'd said, "No, I'd rather not go through that door. I can't see what's behind it"?

But somehow Rebekah saw the upside, the potential. She realized the servant's devotion to God through his words, his actions, and his certainty that this opportunity was God's plan. God must have put a feeling or word of confirmation in her heart. And so, Rebekah said yes—and walked through the door of her future and ours.

Both Matthew and Luke recount that Jesus was a descendant of Jacob—Rebekah and Isaac's son. If Rebekah had stayed put, there would be no Jacob. Which would mean there would also be no Judah, King David, King Solomon, King Hezekiah, or Joseph—the man who married Mary, gave Jesus a name and a home, and saved Jesus from King Herod by moving him to Egypt when He was a baby. I'm so grateful Rebekah was willing to walk through that door. I don't like to imagine what would have happened if she hadn't.

I also don't want to think what would have happened if Brett and I hadn't moved to Oxford. On so many levels, God has blessed us richly here.

As Aslan tells Lucy in C. S. Lewis's novel *Prince Caspian*, "To know what *would* have happened, child? . . . No. Nobody is ever told that. . . . But anyone can find out what *will* happen."[1]

What *will* happen if you walk through that door?

What door is God nudging you toward? What door has He already opened for you that you're standing in front of, deciding if you should cross the threshold? Pursuing that degree? Trying an alternate treatment? Seeking help? Letting go of something that no longer serves you? Starting your own business? Making that call? You'll probably never know what would happen if you don't walk through the door God is inviting you to walk through. But if you say yes? Well, you'll get to see what a good God we have, that He plans beautiful, intricate, personal things for your future. Some you might see right away. And some you might not see until twenty-two years later.

Let's bravely take a step forward, trusting that our mighty God is with us, that His plans for us are perfect, and that He will empower us as we walk through the doors He opens for us.

Walk Through the Door

"I will go," she said. (Genesis 24:58)

- Are there any doors you feel Jesus is calling you to walk through? What are some of the thoughts running through your head about this doorway?
- Imagine for a moment (like Rebekah must have) what cool opportunities potentially lie ahead.
- Close your eyes and flip your questions into a prayer: *Dear Jesus, what do You have in store for me if I say yes? Please help me see the opportunities, not the challenges. Please give me the courage to trust in Your perfect plans and step forward in faith. Amen.*

5

Fight for the Ones You Love

Jochebed

No! No! No! My sock is too bunchy!" my toddler squealed as I slid his shoe on his foot.

I'd never considered the bunchy-ness of socks before, but I understood what he meant—that strange sensation when a sock feels like it's all wadded up inside your shoe. I slipped off his sneaker and the navy-blue sock imprinted with raised letters on the bottom. I took a deep breath and tried to reposition the sock back on his foot. Only to be informed that the other sock was "even more bunchy-er."

That was just his socks.

My now-twenty-two-year-old son experienced all his senses on hyperdrive when he was little. To him, sirens screamed so loudly he'd hold his hands over his ears and squeeze his eyes shut for long after the sirens were out of earshot. The unsettling sensation of having his nails trimmed or the buzz of electric hair clippers could shut him down. One squirt of hand sanitizer seemed as potent as falling in a puddle of pungent perfume. Anything that didn't have an elastic waistband was unbearably uncomfortable. My son's world was overwhelmingly loud and bright and achingly intense.

I was distraught and had no idea how to help him. So I read, googled, spoke to his pediatrician, and prayed like crazy. And although there was no medical "proof," I discovered many moms found success switching their sensory kids to a gluten-free diet. Going gluten-free couldn't hurt us, and even though it might not work, it just might. And therefore, I was willing to try.

But removing gluten from our food supply would be a challenge, to say the least. We ate gluten-packed cereal for breakfast, sandwiches on gluten-y bread for lunch, and pasta or pizza or some kind of wheat product with most dinners. Keep in mind, this was nineteen years ago. Gluten-free wasn't vogue or considered a healthy dietary choice. Restaurants didn't indicate gluten-free choices. Today gluten-free options are easily accessible at grocery stores and online. But in those days, gluten-free items were scarce and challenging to find. Ordering foods on Amazon was not an option yet. This dietary switch was going to be tricky.

I did a major rehaul of our pantry, read every label, and invested time researching and meal prepping. I needed to have gluten-free treats and snacks at the ready in my purse because we ended up at playdates, picnics, and parties where there were no safe options for my boy. It was hard. I was clueless about what I was doing. But I never considered *not* trying it. I loved my son and would do anything to increase his quality of life.

It's what we do for the people we love.

Try our hardest and hit our knees asking God for help where we fall short.

Fortunately, our God sees us when we extend love to the people we care about. Remember, He loves them too. Even more than we do. And where we are weak? God steps in, empowers us, and fills in the gaps we can't fill on our own.

God tells us, "My grace is sufficient for you, for my power is made perfect in weakness" (2 Corinthians 12:9).

And that leads us to Jochebed, a Hebrew woman living under the reign of the Egyptian pharaoh. She married a man from her tribe, the tribe of Levi, and had a baby boy. Sounds so sweet. Except they were enslaved. And there was another hitch. No, her son wasn't sensory or sensitive to gluten—at least not that we know of—but not too long before her baby's birth, Pharaoh ordered his people to throw every newborn Hebrew boy into the Nile River to be drowned (Exodus 1:22).

Jochebed couldn't fathom the thought of her son being slaughtered, so she took action. As we've been talking about, it's what we do for the people we love. For starters, Jochebed hid her baby for three months. Which, if you've ever heard a newborn cry when they're hungry or tired or hungry *and* tired, you have an idea of the enormity of this challenge.

> When she could no longer hide him, she got a basket made of papyrus reeds and waterproofed it with tar and pitch. She put the baby in the basket and laid it among the reeds along the bank of the Nile River. (Exodus 2:3 NLT)

I can't imagine how excruciating it was for Jochebed to set her baby in the basket and kiss her little guy goodbye. She would never get to cuddle him close again, breathe in that soft baby scent of her son. And what if the wrong people found him? Or no one found him? Or the makeshift boat leaked, and he drowned? But it was worth the risk because what if he was saved? Jochebed would need some divine intervention. She believed in the one true God, and although she didn't know what would happen, her faith gave her enough courage to take the plunge.

God saw Jochebed. He saw how much she loved her son and that she would do anything for him. God had incredible plans for that little boy, as He does for all of us (Jeremiah 29:11), and when Jochebed had done all *she* could do, God kept working. Once baby Moses was floating in his basket, he was found rather quickly by, of all people, the pharaoh's daughter—a princess. And even though she was Egyptian and could tell the baby was Hebrew, even though she knew about her dad's law to kill Hebrew baby boys, the Bible tells us the princess felt sorry for the little guy.

This next part of the story blows me away—a little divine icing on the cake, and I am a huge fan of icing.

> The baby's sister [who had been watching from a distance] approached the princess. "Should I go and find one of the Hebrew women to nurse the baby for you?" she asked.
>
> "Yes, do!" the princess replied. So the girl went and called the baby's mother.
>
> "Take this baby and nurse him for me," the princess told the baby's mother. "I will pay you for your help." So the woman took *her* baby home and nursed him. (Exodus 2:7–9 NLT, emphasis mine)

Jochebed got to take Moses back home with her. The son she had just sobbed over setting in a basket she was now able to nurse and snuggle and sing to for years. She even got paid for it. Which certainly wasn't necessary, but being enslaved, this surely added to her family's financial security. God had the exact right person discover Moses in his floating basket. God positioned Moses's sister, Miriam, in just the right place at just the right time, gave her just the right words when speaking to the princess, and gave the princess the perfect response. God gave Jochebed her son back for quite some time. Eventually (the Bible says "when the boy was older"), the princess took Moses to the palace, where he grew up in royalty. God would one day use Moses to lead His people out of slavery and into freedom.

The Bible doesn't mention if Jochebed had any idea what an important role Moses would play in freeing her entire nation. I think it would have, had she known. She just loved her boy, wanted what was best for him, and would do anything for his health and happiness, even if it was the hardest thing she ever had to do.

I bet you do this too. You do the hard things for the people you love, simply because you love them.

I picture Jochebed nursing Moses extra times to keep him quiet, even though he'd just eaten, even though she felt depleted. I imagine her hiding under a blanket or tucked behind a bush with Moses, so no one would hear her son's fussing as she rocked him to sleep. I believe God gave her the endurance and courage to keep at it. The day Jochebed realized her boy was getting too big to hide, I'm guessing God gave her the idea for the basket, and she got to work weaving. Scripture includes the details of how she lined it with pitch to keep it dry and safe inside, and I believe Jochebed did it without hesitation, like a mom on a mission. The clock was ticking and if she was going to save her son she had to move. It wasn't easy, but it was worth it. Where Jochebed hit her limitations, our mighty God went the extra mile, arranging the details, making all the pieces fall into place, and boosting Jochebed with a jolt of bravery to follow through on her plan. This is who our God is. This is what He does.

> The LORD is trustworthy in all he promises,
>   and faithful in all he does.
> The LORD upholds all who fall
>   and lifts up all who are bowed down. . . .
>
> The LORD is near to all who call on him,
>   to all who call on him in truth.
> He fulfills the desires of those who fear him;
>   he hears their cry and saves them.
>   (Psalm 145:13–14, 18–19)

While going gluten-free doesn't come close to what Jochebed was up against, it wasn't easy for me. But God saw me. He must have, because I didn't feel burdened by having to be creative with our cooking. Even juggling four littles, I somehow found extra time to make more things from scratch. An unexpected conversation with a woman I kind-of-sort-of knew revealed she was also trying the gluten-free route for her kids. I believe God gave me this woman at this exact time to compare notes, recipes, and products with. Even though my tendency is to be a pleaser, I never considered caving when my kids and husband complained about our new gluten-free menu. I didn't waver when an extended family member suggested that being sensitive to gluten wasn't a "real thing," that she'd read "eating gluten-free really wasn't healthy." Or when a friend and fellow mom asked, "Why don't you just let your son eat like the other kids?"

I stood firm. I had a resolve that did not come from me. My strength and courage came from the Lord. I did what I could, and God did the rest. He knew where and how I was weak, and what I would need most.

God created my son and had grand plans for him. Going gluten-free during his growing-up years was a gift. About one week into making the dietary switch, I trimmed his fingernails and the whole ordeal was over before either of us knew it. A complete turnaround from the previous thirty-minute ritual. The whole nail-trimming escapade was like night and day.

Experts said it would take approximately thirty days to notice any difference from the dietary shift. But God swept in and gave us speedy results, encouragement to keep going. Getting dressed became a breeze. Bunchy socks were no longer problematic. Noises were less jarring. My son's quality of life immensely improved. He smiled more and struggled less.

I can't take credit for this change. I didn't know anything about sensory processing disorder—having a hypersensitivity to your five senses—or about eating gluten-free. God put these concepts in front of me. God gave me resources to learn. He gave me boldness to try and then to stick with the countercultural move. It was a huge ordeal for me at the time, but I know our switch to gluten-free was such a small struggle—seemingly nothing compared to the women around me.

I sit on the sidelines, watching wonderful women do brave, unprecedented things for the people they love. One friend goes to the nursing home every week and paints the fingernails of her mother-in-law, who suffers from Alzheimer's. Another friend, a single mom, started her own business, enabling her to set her own hours so she can both provide for and spend time with her son. One friend recently decided to homeschool her daughters even though it was not her passion and incredibly inconvenient. But the situation at her girls' school had gone awry, and she wanted better for them. Another friend cooks extra every week so she can provide meals for an ailing friend. A couple we know adopted a baby girl and were asked on the spot if they would also adopt her older brother. They said yes and brought both kids home.

Loving others sacrificially isn't easy.

But it's how Jesus loves us and how He calls us to love each other. When we are willing, He gives us the tools we need to make our loads feel lighter—like we can carry them with His help. Sure, we'll have days when we're exhausted, say something (or lots of things) we wish we could stuff back in our mouths, throw our hands in the air, or run low on resources. But I've seen God provide the financially struggling woman with an unexpected check, the caretaker a much-needed break, the foster mom a flexible work schedule, or one worried mama a princess to fish her beloved boy out of the river.

> Loving others sacrificially isn't easy.
> But when we are willing, He gives
> us the tools we need.

You get the picture.

Jesus floods us with inexplicable energy, strength, bravery, and peace. When we can't do it on our own, He will help us discover resources, bite our tongues, or find a way.

God sees my friends and the love they so freely dish out. God saw Jochebed, so willing to save her son that she would first hide then let go of Moses to protect his life. God saw me, the girl who always does a nosedive for the bread basket, trying to figure out an entirely different food strategy for our family. He sees you and all the little and big things, the sacrifices and bold choices you're making for the people you love. They are making a difference.

I can't promise that your child will run for president or find a cure for cancer or even be healed. I can't promise that the budget won't be tight or that the people you love will acknowledge or appreciate your kindness. But I can promise that, like God saw Jochebed, He sees you and will empower you. He'll provide a way when you feel like you're out of options. He'll step in when you meet the end of your rope, and turn your love into something exponentially more powerful and beautiful.

Fight for the Ones You Love

The LORD is near to all who call on him,
  to all who call on him in truth.
He fulfills the desires of those who fear him;
  he hears their cry and saves them.
                          (Psalm 145:18–19)

- Are you facing challenges trying to care for someone you love? Have you talked to God about this situation? Ask Him to make you brave, like Jochebed, to fight for the people you love.
- Write out the verses above in your journal. Then live it out.
  Call on God.
  Ask Him to fulfill your desires, to help where you need help, to step in where you can't go any further, to lift you up where you are weary, to shower the special person you love with blessings in ways you cannot. Thank Him for His constant, faithful love.

6

Sing

Miriam

Friday mornings at our house are wild. At six forty-five they start showing up. College girls in cozy hoodies and leggings. College boys with bed head, wearing graphic tees. They pile their shoes by our front door—Crocs, Converse, and the like. Most help themselves to a cup of coffee from the pot on the counter. Some give me hugs or smile and say, "Good morning, Mrs. Smith." Many shuffle through the kitchen, half asleep—it's extremely early for college students—and find a seat on our caramel-colored couch or the carpet. They're all here for one reason. To sing to the Lord.

College is stressful. These kids feel the weight of it. Struggling with their identities. Shouldering the pressure to perform. Trying to keep close to Jesus while immersed in a party culture. Living away from home with people they've never lived with before. Feeling a need to look a certain way and wear that brand of sunglasses and sneakers and have an internship or job for next summer already lined up. Juggling friends, family, coursework, a part-time job to help pay for school, student organizations, and their faith. But they come here on Friday mornings to worship.

Why? Because worship reminds us who our God is. It reminds us not only that is God all-powerful but that He uses that power and might to fight for us. It reminds us that God is faithful—that He promises to never leave us. And when we remember all that, it flips a switch in our brains. We start remembering all the things God has done for us, all the ways He's saved the day, showed up just in time, gotten us through a storm. Our problems seem smaller. We remember we don't have to do it all on our own. Most importantly we remember that we are loved.

Worship reminds us that not only is God all-powerful but that He uses that power and might to fight for us.

Our family room is full of fifty to seventy-five college kids singing their hearts out Friday mornings. They belt out how great our God is, that He is a waymaker, rescuer, redeemer, lover, defender, that He's worthy of all our praise and worship. They sing songs of thanks and invite Jesus into the room, their hearts, their lives. There is a tangible presence. There is joy and love and hope. And it fills up the very air in our house.

Miriam knew all about the power of worship.

Quick reminder: Miriam was Moses's big sister. Our mighty God gave Miriam the courage to bravely approach the Egyptian princess and say, "Hey, looks like you could use some help raising the little guy. I know just the lady." Without Miriam, we don't know if Jochebed would have gotten those precious years back with Moses.

Well, bold little Miriam grew up into prophet Miriam and played a key role in leading the Israelites out of slavery in Egypt.

God reminds us, "For I brought you out of Egypt and redeemed you from slavery. I sent Moses, Aaron, and Miriam to help you" (Micah 6:4 NLT).

And when the millions (yes, millions) of Israelites crossed the Red Sea to safety and God brought the waves crashing down on Pharaoh's army, which was in hot pursuit, Miriam whipped out her tambourine and led all the women in worship.

And Miriam sang this song:
   "Sing to the LORD,
      for he has triumphed gloriously;
   he has hurled both horse and rider
      into the sea."
                                    (Exodus 15:21 NLT)

The Israelites were free. God destroyed their enemies. Miriam didn't want anyone to take credit for this themselves. She didn't want this historic, triumphant moment to go unnoticed. She wanted to celebrate big-time. She wanted everyone to get in on it. And she wanted to give God the glory—all the glory.

Sure, the Israelites had abruptly left behind their homes and most of their possessions, as well as the way of life they'd always known. They were currently on the other side of a sea they'd never crossed, in a land they knew nothing about. Women lugged babies, blankets, and bags stuffed with necessities. Men toted as much food and supplies as they could carry. None of them knew what was next. God had guaranteed them the "promised land," but where was it? How far? When would they get there? What would it be like?

No one knew. There was reason to fear and worry, but for right now, they were going to praise God for what He had done. Miriam made sure of it. She didn't need a stage or a mic or a band. She didn't need to rehearse or have perfect lighting. Miriam just needed to praise God—she knew it would make all the difference. She'd seen God at work before, when He saved her baby brother in that basket. God had taught Miriam that He would give her exactly what she needed to be brave. She knew worshiping would help her people hold this moment in their hearts and prepare them for what lay ahead. She also knew they should thank God for His rescue, for answering their prayers, for keeping His promises.

Deborah and Mary knew this too. These women also sang beautiful songs of praise to God that are documented in the Bible (Judges 5; Luke 1:46–55). Miriam, Deborah, and Mary all knew that through worship, they could drop their concerns at God's feet and for a moment be fully aware of His goodness.

As worship leader Jonathan Helser says, "When you sing, heaven invades the earth."[1]

The college students at Friday Morning Worship sing so that heaven can invade their lives on this campus. Their worries and concerns still exist. They still have unknowns about their futures. A lot of them are carrying some pretty heavy baggage. But on Friday mornings? They thank God for who He is, for all He's done, for the ways He's shown up for them. They hand over their questions and uncertainties to Jesus, lay them at His feet, and trust Him to move. They raise their voices as Miriam did. And as the psalmist instructs, they "shout for joy to the LORD. . . . Worship the LORD with gladness; come before him with joyful songs" (Psalm 100:1–2).

It's not just the college kids who get something out of Friday Morning Worship. There are some community members who also attend. And because we host, I get the privilege of being a part of it too. You can usually find me crisscross applesauce on the floor, singing and swaying and often weeping. An hour of organic, unplugged worship is Good. For. My. Soul. There is no agenda. It's not a pregame warm-up for a sermon. There are no members or visitors or denominations or doctrines. No dress codes. Pajama pants are all the rage. It's just a time to celebrate and remember all that the Lord has done and is doing, like filling our home with students seeking Jesus and blessing us with a home where this can take place. It's a time to drop my to-dos and worries at the feet of Jesus and remember who He is, how mighty He is, how He gives me the strength and courage to do what He calls me to, and how deeply He loves me. It's a reminder that God has triumphed gloriously again and again—at the Red Sea, on the cross, in my life, in this room—and that He'll do it again.

Sing

Shout for joy to the LORD, all the earth.
Worship the LORD with gladness;
come before him with joyful songs.
(Psalm 100:1–2)

- There are so many ways to integrate worship into your life. Music isn't the only way, but for now, let's focus on that. If you're musical like Miriam, why not write, sing, or play a song of thanks to God on your instrument of choice today.
- If you're not musical, like me, play some worship tunes (there's a playlist at the back of this book to get you started) and sing along while you commute, cook, carpool, or cut the grass. Take note of how you felt before, during, and after worship.

7

Do the Crazy Thing

Rahab

Have you ever been in a situation where you were living your life, minding your own business, and suddenly felt called to take action?

You might have been in the middle of something else. You might have felt completely unqualified for the crisis at hand, but you felt God nudging and realized standing by was not the right answer. Sometimes there's an obvious way to help. You see someone with a flat tire on the side of the road and you call roadside assistance. Or maybe the person in front of you in line is a dollar short, and you hand them one of yours. But sometimes you're not even sure what you should or could do—and then God whispers something outlandish. And you do the crazy thing.

That's what happened to Rahab.

It wasn't uncommon for men Rahab didn't know to stop by and spend the night. Her home was an inn, and she was a prostitute. But one night, two Israelite spies came to her home. There had been talk in town about the Israelites. The God they worshiped sounded incredibly powerful, which had created an uneasy buzz in the city. If those Israelites showed up, what would happen? And here two of them were in her house. Rahab felt a tug in her heart to help them. Which seemed crazy. They were the enemy. She could be killed for such a thing. She had zero experience in espionage. She was not a trained soldier. As a woman at that time, she would have been uneducated. She also had a racy reputation.

But God didn't care. He made Rahab. He loved her. And God wanted to invite her into something incredible. The one true God of Israel nudged Rahab and showed her what needed to be done, even though it sounded outrageous. And she did the crazy thing—hiding and helping her town's enemies. Even when the king got wind of the spies and came looking for them at Rahab's place.

> But [Rahab] had taken the two men and hidden them. She said, "Yes, the men came to me, but I did not know where they had come from. At dusk, when it was time to close the city gate, they left. I don't know which way they went. Go after them quickly. You may catch up with them." (But she had taken them up to the roof and hidden them under the stalks of flax she had laid out on the roof.) So, the men set out in pursuit of the spies on the road that leads to the fords of the Jordan, and as soon as the pursuers had gone out, the gate was shut. (Joshua 2:4–7)

What motivated Rahab to the wild and dangerous act of lying to the king's men? She understood who God was. And no matter how outlandish His request, Rahab wanted to obey it.

> Before the spies lay down for the night, she went up on the roof and said to them, "I know that the Lord has given you this land and that a great fear of you has fallen on us, so that all who live in this country are melting in fear because of you. We have heard how the Lord dried up the water of the Red Sea for you when you came out of Egypt, and what you did to Sihon and Og, the two kings of the Amorites east of the Jordan, whom you completely destroyed. When we heard of

it, our hearts melted in fear and everyone's courage failed because of you, for the LORD your God is God in heaven above
and on the earth below. (Joshua 2:8–11)

How did pagan Rahab know about God? The same way most of us
do at first. She heard stories about Him, heard people talking about
the God of the Israelites, and He sounded incredible. Drying up the
Red Sea. Destroying powerful kings. Caring so intentionally for His
people. This God was someone Rahab could believe in. God stirred
her heart and let her know somewhere deep inside that He was more
powerful than heaven or earth and that whatever He was up to, she
should be a part of it.

Rahab hadn't been brought up in the faith, didn't have training in
being a secret agent or in military operations. Rahab didn't have time
to organize a plan. It was a now-or-never invitation. But our mighty
God spoke to Rahab, and Rahab listened to His still, small voice and
bravely acted on it.

What Rahab *did* have was knowledge of her city. She knew how
it worked. Not because she'd studied it or been on city council, but
simply because she lived there. And that was all she needed to come up
with a strategy on the spot and execute it. God gave Rahab the precise
knowledge necessary to help the spies. They didn't know there was flax
on the roof they could crawl under to be concealed. They didn't know
they should hide in the hills. They didn't know three days would be
the right amount of time. But Rahab knew all those things. God fully
equipped her.

And He equips you and me too. God invites us to speak up and
gives us the right words. He has us leave a blanket in our back seat,
then invites us to share it with someone who's shivering. He prompts
us to ask someone a question that leads them to share a dream or
struggle that they really needed to voice. God invites us into remarkable work. Let's be part of it. Let's do the thing—even when it seems
crazy—when the Holy Spirit gives us that Almighty nudge.

"Will you do it for Me?" God asks.

God asked my friend Jessica to do something crazy. She was staying out of town with her in-laws and dropped by a farmers' market to buy tomatoes. The man working told her they were going out of business. The owner, who was his best friend, had passed away the day before. This man holding down the fort was devastated, didn't have workers, and wasn't sure how they would ever sell the existing produce to pay their debts. Jessica had a wallet full of money she'd just gotten for her birthday and heard God say, *Buy it all.*

What?

> God invites us into remarkable work.
> Let's be part of it. Let's do the thing—
> even when it seems crazy.

Jessica didn't know these people. She doesn't have a business degree or expertise or experience in saving a farmer's market. She couldn't use an entire store of produce. But God gave Jessica exactly what she needed—timing, cash, a car, and an invitation. She bought every last pumpkin and squash, set it on her sister-in-law's lawn, and posted in the local Facebook group that there was free produce for the taking. By early afternoon, everything had been claimed by people who couldn't afford groceries, schoolteachers who wanted to provide crafts for their students, and locals who were amazed that someone was supporting the farming family they'd known all their lives. Jessica got to shine light on an entire community she didn't even know. Not because she planned an outreach, promoted an event, or set out to pay tribute to a local legend, but because she obediently RSVP'd to God's wild invitation and used what He gave her.

Jessica posted on social media a picture of her car filled to the gills with gourds, with the caption *Do the crazy thing.*

God calls us to outrageous things. Time and time again. And He gives us exactly what we need to do them—some flax, birthday money, whatever—then He does something more than we can ever hope or imagine with our obedience.

The spies who Rahab helped escape returned to Joshua, and then all kinds of things went down. God parted the Jordan River (probably forty feet deep)[1] for the Israelites to cross on dry land. The Israelite men all got circumcised. *Ouch.* And rested. And healed. The Israelites celebrated Passover. And then Joshua led his army on the famous seven-day march around the walls of Jericho. On the seventh time around the city on the seventh day, Joshua ordered his army, "Shout! For the LORD has given you the city! The city and all that is in it are to be devoted to the LORD. Only Rahab the prostitute and all who are with her in her house shall be spared, because she hid the spies we sent" (Joshua 6:16–17).

And the walls came tumbling down.

The forty thousand men in the Israelite army had seen miracles, had surgery, celebrated a festival, and were currently conquering a city. And in the moment before the city walls crashed Joshua said, "Make sure you take care of Rahab."

What? Because that's how God responds to our obedience. Faithfully and abundantly.

Just before the entire town and everything in it was destroyed, the two spies took off to Rahab's house and rescued her and her entire family. Hundreds of years later, the author of the book of Hebrews recited a list of historical figures who exhibited remarkable faith, saying, "By faith the prostitute Rahab, because she welcomed the spies, was not killed with those who were disobedient" (11:31). She was called out by name on this impressive list of the faithful.

Rahab did what she could. She didn't have prestige, power, or position—she was a prostitute who lived in an enemy town. But she had some straw, a roof, and a belief that God was mighty, and she accepted God's invitation.

That's all we need. Not necessarily the straw or a roof, but whatever God has already put in front of us.

God loves inviting us into His work. He doesn't need us. He's God. He could have made Israel's spies invisible or hid them somewhere else. God could have funded that produce in other ways. But then Rahab and Jessica would have missed out on all the fun.

Rahab got to see her family saved. Jessica got to tell the farmer's best friend about Jesus and heard story after story of appreciation from locals. We'll probably never see the full effect of our acts of obedience. Rahab died without knowing her name would be recorded in history. She didn't know she'd be an example to women from all walks of life of the mighty things they can do for God. Jessica didn't get to see the smiles on the faces of the students painting pumpkins or taste the tangy soup prepared with free tomatoes and onions. She left town and won't ever hear the conversations about the day a yard was filled with free veggies and how it changed someone's day, week, or month.

But Rahab and Jessica did the crazy thing when God asked them to. God gave them everything they needed.

And then He used it mightily.

What crazy thing is God calling you to today? What's stopping you from doing it?

Do the Crazy Thing

But [Rahab] had taken the two men and hidden them. (Joshua 2:4)

- Has something like this happened to you? God calling you to do something outlandish like He did with Rahab? If so, did you do it? Why or why not?
- Is there something wild God is calling you into in this season?
- Write out a prayer thanking God for inviting you into His work and asking Him to give you ears to hear His promptings and the courage to say yes to the crazy thing.

8

Be the Change
Deborah

When I went to pick up my freshman daughter, the senior soccer players had their car trunks open, tailgating in the parking lot. Tunes playing. Mouths full of pizza they'd had delivered.

That day, after practice, was the first of many ice baths sprinkled intermittently in the girls' rigorous routine of grueling summer practices. The "bathtubs" were giant garbage cans filled with ice and water in which the girls took turns soaking their overworked leg muscles in the school parking lot.

Were all the girls finished and just socializing now? I wondered. Where was my daughter? I looked around the parking lot but didn't see her. I didn't want to embarrass her, so I texted, *Are you almost done?*

Sorry. Only the seniors are done. It'll probably be another half hour. At least.

What? I wondered. It wasn't my daughter's fault, but running a half hour late was inconvenient for anyone picking up their girl. She was right about the "at least" part. I ended up waiting over an hour.

"Sorry," my daughter said, sounding as annoyed as I was as she climbed in the passenger seat.

"What happened?" I asked.

"The seniors literally had us do everything. They said, 'Go get the ice!' but none of us knew where the ice was. They said, 'Get the tubs!' and we didn't know where to find those either. When we asked, they just told us to find it." She fastened her seat belt with a click and took a long drink from her water bottle. "They just ordered us around, and no one would help us find or do anything, and then they made us go last." She shook her head.

"And they ordered pizza?" I asked.

"Yeah." My girl's voice was full of frustration. "Just for them. They thought that was pretty funny." She raised her eyebrows.

There was a distinct culture in place with the girls' soccer team. It was way more than the ice baths. It also included a week of "team bonding" every August, which pushed the limits of new players—not on the field, but by daring them to participate in late-night escapades and outrageous stunts such as skinny-dipping and extreme TP-ing of other students' homes. All to "show loyalty" to the team. There was an attitude of intimidating younger girls, "putting them in their place," and "making them earn respect" instead of welcoming them. Freshmen were expected to clean up balls and cones after practices and games. Seniors earned elite rights, including bossing the younger girls around. It's how things were. The coach supported and encouraged this behavior. It was the only thing the older girls had ever known. They paid their dues as freshmen and worked their way up to senior status.

There were good things too. Great things. The team was extremely talented and had successful season after successful season, with many players moving on to compete at the college level. Dedicated parents organized fundraisers that provided quality training, healthy meals and snacks before and after games, and snazzy gear for a girls' sport that was not exactly the school's top priority. To be on this soccer team held weight. The team was a well-oiled machine with a history of excellence. It was full of traditions and expectations, but over the years the culture had gotten out of hand.

My daughter thought the same. She endured freshman year. Played hard. Did what she was told. Picked up and set up gear without

complaint. Enlisted friends to boldly say no with her to the inappropriate expectations at team bonding. And on the first practice of her
sophomore year, she made it a point to say hello to every freshman
even though the juniors and seniors discouraged it. On their first ice
bath day as sophomores, my daughter and her friends helped get the
ice and the tubs, showing new girls where they were stored. My girl
and her friends helped clean up, while the juniors and seniors acted
like confused spectators.

My daughter remembered how it felt to not have the older girls
care who you were, and she vowed not to let anyone else feel that way.
The coaching staff changed, and by the time she was a senior, she and
her friends had flipped the culture upside down. Freshmen were welcomed. The hazing was gone. Senior week became a team dinner, a fun
scavenger hunt around town, and a service project. Everyone helped set
up before and clean up after practices and games, even seniors—often
seniors. Instead of a hierarchy, they became a team. And that team
was still super talented. By the time my daughter graduated, this *new*
culture was all the existing soccer players had ever known. It hadn't
been easy, but the culture had been changed. Oh, and five of the eight
girls from her graduating class went on to play in college.

When we first meet Deborah in the Bible, her people are also living
in a harsh culture. They had been oppressed by the commander of
King Jabin of Hazor's army, Sisera, for twenty years.

But God came to Deborah and told her He would give her victory
over cruel Sisera. He even told her how to do it. Deborah was excited
for there to be a change, and she was obedient when God asked her to
be the catalyst.

> She sent for Barak son of Abinoam from Kedesh in Naphtali
> and said to him, "The LORD, the God of Israel, commands
> you: 'Go, take with you ten thousand men of Naphtali and
> Zebulun and lead them up to Mount Tabor. I will lead Si-
> sera, the commander of Jabin's army, with his chariots and his
> troops to the Kishon River and give him into your hands.'"
> (Judges 4:6–7)

Deborah listened to God, approached Barak, one of her military leaders, and gave him marching orders. But Barak balked at Deborah's request. "If you don't go with me, I won't go," he said (4:8).

There is almost always resistance when we try to change things. Even when we know we're doing the right thing. Even when we hear directly from God on how to go about doing it. My daughter met resistance. There were days she felt alone. Days when the upperclassmen laughed at her and her friends, when it would have been easier to have the freshmen haul the ice or lug the cones than doing it herself. That team-bonding week freshman year when she refused to participate in one of the activities, when she suggested doing something else altogether even though things had always been done a certain way, took courage and resolve. But my daughter knew in her heart what Jesus would do, and that was love her teammates—all of them—and you don't force people you love to embarrass themselves or put themselves in bad situations.

> There is almost always resistance when we try to change things. Even when we hear directly from God on how to go about doing it.

Deborah also knew what God wanted her to do, so she didn't let the force of the enemy's army or Barak's hesitancy deter her.

> "Certainly I will go with you," said Deborah. "But because of the course you are taking, the honor will not be yours, for the LORD will deliver Sisera into the hands of a woman." (Judges 4:9)

That day every one of Sisera's men were killed, and so was Sisera. Deborah and Barak were victorious and broke into song. Their song praised God for their victory and can be found in Judges 5. After the last lyrics of the song are recorded, the author of Judges stated, "Then the land had peace forty years" (verse 31).

Deborah took her people from two decades of oppression to four decades of peace. How? By being in close contact with God. Talking to Him on a regular basis and listening to His voice. By acting on God's prompts. Even when it went against the crowd, against the norm. When God told Deborah to do something, she didn't question it. She just did it. When it didn't go exactly as planned, Deborah didn't care. She took the next step and the one after that. And when the culture flipped from oppression to peace, Deborah gave God all the glory.

We're all immersed in multiple subcultures. The subcultures in our communities, neighborhoods, cities, states, and countries. Living in Mississippi is way different from living in New Jersey. There are different dress codes, slang words, accents, foods, and paces of life. We have the cultures of our extended families, dinner tables, play groups, swimming pools, work environments, churches, team and client meetings, committees or boards, small groups, or Bible studies. Each has their own feeling to them, different protocols. Some of these groups we are immersed in simply because of where we were born or who we were born to. Others we've chosen to be a part of.

And because these subcultures are part of this world, they're probably not all run like Jesus would run them—with acceptance, love, kindness, fairness, and honesty. But God calls us to a higher standard than that of the world.

> And what does the LORD require of you?
> To act justly and to love mercy
>   and to walk humbly with your God.
>   (Micah 6:8)

Are there ways we can step in and step up, or maybe even step out, to make positive changes in the communities where we live?

Can we be the ones to insist we start praying as a family or that we intentionally seek diverse members of our board or club to better represent God's kingdom? Can we suggest a more ethical way of handling customers or billing so it honors God? Can we stretch out our arms to welcome newcomers? Is there a way we can better show appreciation for our subordinates?

It starts with God. He puts us all in positions to do His work and share His love. But then we need to act. Like Deborah did. Like my daughter did. Even when it's hard. Even when no one else seems to be willing to help. Even when we have to stand up to a powerful military leader or some sassy seniors. Because when God empowers us, we can do mighty things. We can change the way the system looks. We can take down an evil ruler. We can end oppression. We can make change for good. All in the name of Jesus.

Are you ready?

Be the Change

And what does the LORD require of you?
To act justly and to love mercy
and to walk humbly with your God.
(Micah 6:8)

- Is there a culture you're immersed in that could better glorify God's kingdom?
- If none comes to mind, take ten minutes to talk to God about this. Maybe jot down some of the subcultures you're a part of. See if you think of anything that feels off. Ask Jesus what He would like for you to be doing, how you might be able to make a change.
- If you know God disapproves of a certain subculture you're in, ask Him how you can be inspired by Deborah and start to change that culture for good. Commit to making one step this week and another next week.

9

Get Your Brave On

Jael

My friend Kristin was diagnosed with pancreatic cancer in September. In March she sent me a text: *I would never wish a cancer diagnosis on anyone. But I would never give up the lessons and perspective it brings. I feel so energized and on fire.*

This message was in a series of texts in which Kristin told me about an amazing faith-based organization that encourages and prays for people with cancer. She sent me a copy of their Prayer for the Sick, which states the devil is defeated and victory is ours because Jesus shed His blood on the cross for us (amen!). And if you knew Kristin, you would not be surprised to hear that she wasn't just being encouraged by this ministry; she wanted to volunteer to help them help others. I could write an entire book about the conversations Kristin and I had over lunch and on walks or over texts or phone calls from September to May. Usually, Kristin was sharing praise for God's love, angels she was certain He had sent her, or a new doctor who was "very encouraging." Even amid difficult treatment or while in pain, she'd say she was "feeling positive and unafraid" or "feeling great." Kristin went to be with the Lord in May. But, dang, she went bravely.

A friend shared at Kristin's funeral that in Kristin's last couple of days on earth she said, "I don't want to die. I want to be here for my boys and grow old with my husband. But I'm not afraid. I feel so much peace. I'm going to fight cancer like crazy, but I know everything will be okay."

Kristin was smiling and singing and fighting and praising Jesus and making everyone she encountered feel loved and special to the very end.

I want to be brave like that. Fearless.

I bet you have some brave friends too.

There is a woman who lived thousands of years ago who should be the poster girl for bravery. Her name is Jael.

Stay with me for some brief backstory.

For twenty years, King Jabin had cruelly oppressed the Israelites. They cried out to the Lord, and God heard His people. God instructed His prophet Deborah to fight the king's army commanded by Sisera. You might remember these folks from the previous chapter. Deborah instructed Barak to gather ten thousand men to attack Sisera and his army of nine hundred chariots. Like most bullies, at the sign of a real threat, Sisera ran away. Here's where Jael makes her entrance.

> Sisera, meanwhile, fled on foot to the tent of Jael, the wife of Heber the Kenite, because there was an alliance between Jabin king of Hazor and the family of Heber the Kenite.
>
> Jael went out to meet Sisera and said to him, "Come, my lord, come right in. Don't be afraid." So he entered her tent, and she covered him with a blanket. (Judges 4:17–18)

All right, let's stop here for a minute. Jael was a woman by herself in a tent thousands of years ago. I'll say that if a man was running on foot in my neighborhood and I was home alone, I wouldn't step out of my house and invite him inside for all the cookie dough in the world. But in Bible times? Men weren't allowed in women's tents at all. Jael's actions are outrageous.

When Sisera heard her invitation, he probably thought he'd gotten the biggest break of his life. But instead of being humble or expressing gratitude, Sisera stepped in, took full advantage of the situation, and treated Jael as his servant, insisting, "Get me a drink." And "Stand there." And "Answer this way." But watch what Jael did.

> "I'm thirsty," he said. "Please give me some water." She opened a skin of milk, gave him a drink, and covered him up.
>
> "Stand in the doorway of the tent," he told her. "If someone comes by and asks you, 'Is anyone in there?' say 'No.'"
>
> But Jael, Heber's wife, picked up a tent peg and a hammer and went quietly to him while he lay fast asleep, exhausted. She drove the peg through his temple into the ground, and he died.
>
> Just then Barak came by in pursuit of Sisera, and Jael went out to meet him. "Come," she said, "I will show you the man you're looking for." So he went in with her, and there lay Sisera with the tent peg through his temple—dead. (Judges 4:19–22)

It's so gruesome. But it's in the Bible. And as I was saying before: Jael equals poster girl for bravery. Sisera was a warrior, a commander of thousands of men for the evil enemy. He was strong and armed. Imagine lulling a man like that to sleep with some warm milk, giving him the guest bed and a blankie, and then killing him with something sharp lying around your home. Jael appears in these verses of the Bible, plus in Deborah and Barak's victory song where they sing, "Most blessed of women be Jael," and then detail her milk-bringing, hammer-hitting acts of bravery (Judges 5:24).

How did Jael muster up the courage to step out of her tent? To speak to the fleeing commander? To come up with a plan so fast? To not let him see the angst and fear on her face as she offered him milk and a place to sleep, knowing what she planned to do? To tiptoe around her tent grabbing a tent peg and hammer, knowing at any second Sisera could wake and see her? To take the action that took down the enemy?

Because our mighty God was with her and made her brave.

God gave Jael an opportunity when Sisera came by, and she seized it. If Jael's voice wobbled or her hand shook, I picture God steadying her. I imagine God whispering, "You can do it. I'm here with you. Act fast. It's now or never. You've got this." And Jael obeyed.

Earlier Barak told Deborah he wouldn't go to fight Sisera and his army unless Deborah went with him. "No problem," Deborah explained, "but you're not going to get the victory today. That honor will go to a woman" (Judges 4:8–9, my paraphrase). That woman was Jael. How did Deborah know this in advance? She was God's prophet, meaning God told Deborah things that should be done and things that *would* happen. Jael taking down Sisera was God's plan before the battle started. God empowered and nudged her, and Jael obediently acted on God's promptings.

My friend Kristin was brave. Jael was rock-star brave. And Jesus calls you and me to be brave too. This isn't something just for women in the Bible or the friends we admire. Courage is ours for the taking, not because we're superheroes, but because the Lord is with us. Because God plans wonderful things beyond our imagination that often take some bravery on our part to come to fruition.

> Be strong and courageous. (Joshua 1:6)
> Be strong and very courageous. (verse 7)
> Have I not commanded you? Be strong and courageous. (verse 9)

I love that God told Joshua three times in only seven sentences to be strong and courageous—like Joshua needed that reinforcement and repetition, because I need it too.

> ## Courage is ours for the taking, not because we're superheroes, but because the Lord is with us.

I need to be brave when I walk in for another mammogram. My family has a history of breast cancer, and I'm the gal the mammographer keeps inviting back every six months. Not because I'm so fun to be with, but because there always appears to be something suspicious on my scans.

I need to be courageous to set my own boundaries to protect myself from someone who has deeply hurt me and has been a serious subject of conversation with my counselor.

What do you need to be brave about?

In a recent conversation I had with my friend Barb Roose, she talked about how sometimes the most courageous thing we can do is say, "For the next hour I'm going to be brave enough to . . ." She and I chatted about ways we might finish that statement. For the next hour I'm going to be brave enough to make that phone call, resist that temptation, get out of bed, research how to do that thing, send the email or text, say no, share a struggle with a friend, take care of my body. Sometimes something like fighting cancer or taking down an enemy warrior seems too big. But saying "For the next hour I'm going to be brave enough to look for something positive about my journey" or "I'm going to be brave enough to offer this man some milk" feels doable, possible. And that brave thing puts you in position to do the next brave thing.

Kristin couldn't have been so brave and joyful the last eight months of her life, she couldn't have made such an incredible impact on others, if she hadn't clung to Jesus. She held on so tightly to Him and took one day, one treatment at a time.

See, God didn't instruct Joshua to "drum up some courage" or "put on his brave face" or to "buck up, buttercup." Nope. He said, "Be strong and courageous, for the LORD your God will be with you wherever you go." Jael had this figured out. The only way she could have invited Sisera in, lulled him to sleep, and driven in that tent peg was because she knew God was with her. Our mighty God was giving her the courage she needed. And as a result, she could be brave.

That's the key. The Lord will be with you and me wherever we go. Jesus promised it.

> And surely I am with you always, to the very end of the age.
> (Matthew 28:20)

And because of that, because Jesus is with us, we can be strong and courageous. We can do hard things. Big things and little things. Things that don't feel brave to others but for us require loads of courage. Things that feel brave to everyone, like Jael with that tent peg. You and me? We can be brave, one step at a time, for the next hour, and the one after that, because our loving God is with us and will never leave our sides.

Get Your Brave On

> Have I not commanded you? Be strong and courageous. Do not be afraid; do not be discouraged, for the LORD your God will be with you wherever you go. (Joshua 1:9)

- What's something that feels overwhelming today?
- Write down something brave you can do for the next hour and something brave you can do later this week.
- Ask God to remind you that He is with you. That He will never leave you. That you don't have to be brave by yourself, but that just like He did for Jael, He will give you the courage you need.

10

Forge Friendships
Ruth

One December some important emails went straight to my spam. They were from someone named Amy who was assigned as the editor on my first book. I got a note from the overseeing editor asking if I'd received Amy's emails and urging me to respond. I hadn't and was mortified. This was my first book deal. I had zero idea what I was doing but wanted to make a good impression. I wanted Amy and her boss to like and approve of me, to think I was talented and professional, and here I was, not even answering emails.

I dug through my spam folder, found Amy's messages, made profuse apologies to both women, and then made sure Amy's contact info was marked as important in my email server.

Amy was gracious and laughed the whole thing off. We worked through my first novel together. Soon after, I was blessed to get an offer for two more novels in the series, and Amy was assigned to edit both. Through our flurry of email exchanges while finessing three novels, we discovered we both love Jack Johnson, chocolate, coffee, mascara, our husbands and kids, being inspired, books, words, and mostly, Jesus. Some people you just really hit it off with.

A year and a half later Amy, who lived in Tennessee, reached out to say she was on a family adventure just an hour from my house. We met at Panera with my two toddlers in tow, and over thick, frothy mochas we had our first in-person conversation, but we felt like old friends. I messaged Amy afterward thanking her for taking time to meet with me. *I love knowing you're out there—an amazing mom, writer, and Christian—to turn to when I have questions, gripes, ideas. I'm certain the good Lord above has brought us together. He's pretty cool like that.*

Amy replied, *God knows when we find each other, we find strength, comfort, and wisdom to better do His work. And I'm glad He did. :)*

Eighteen years later, we both have new email addresses. Our kids have grown up. We've attended and spoken at multiple writing conferences together. During those conferences we've had sleepovers everywhere from funky Airbnb rentals to each other's homes and even my mom's house. Combined we've written over eighty books (for the record, seventy of them are Amy's!). Amy is one of my very best and dearest friends. We've shared stories, tears, hugs, giggles, and so many mochas.

Amy prayed with me when my father-in-law passed away, when the publisher I was writing fiction for stopped publishing fiction, when my big kids were looking for the right colleges, when I had to go in for yet another mammogram. I've talked through every single writing idea I've had with her. Three of my books could not have happened if it weren't for introductions Amy made for me. She's talked to me on the phone while tears poured down my face, because I just wasn't sure what God wanted me to do. She's sent me a million care packages stuffed with goodies ranging from scratch-and-sniff stamps to a graphic tee that says Aslan's famous quote, "Courage, dear heart."[1] She's sent me so many cards that my kids recognize her handwriting. It's Amy, who in the midst of a family crisis of her own, texts me that she's praying for *my* daughter who has strep throat.

Basically, I can't imagine life without her.

Do you have a friend like that?

Navigating life with a true, loyal, trustworthy friend is priceless. These friendships have been critical to the life of women dating all the way back to the Old Testament. In fact, an entire book of the Bible is dedicated to the story of a woman named Ruth and her friendship with her mother-in-law Naomi. Both widowed and with uncertainty looming, with the help of God these women clung to and helped each other step into a new future.

When Ruth's husband (Naomi's son) died, Naomi, who was already a widow, suggested Ruth go back home and live under her father's roof and protection. But Ruth loved Naomi and instead chose to stick with her.

> But Ruth replied, "Don't urge me to leave you or to turn back from you. Where you go I will go, and where you stay I will stay. Your people will be my people and your God my God. Where you die I will die, and there I will be buried." (Ruth 1:16–17)

What an incredible testimony of friendship.

And what a powerful testimony of God's mighty love at work. Ruth must have seen how dedicated Naomi's family was to the Lord, how important and integral He was to their daily lives, what a difference He made for them. God used all this to stir in Ruth's heart a desire to follow Him and the courage to step into a ride-or-die friendship with her mother-in-law.

Ruth left her home, her family, her customs, her other friends, the things she'd known all her life, and traveled with Naomi to Bethlehem—not a fun road trip on a sunny day with the top down and tunes playing, but approximately a weeklong journey through rugged terrain on foot. Do you have many friends you'd do that with? Who'd do that for you?

Once in Bethlehem, what are two gals to do? If you've ever moved, you can relate to the challenges of a new town: Where is there a decent, safe, affordable place to live? Is there a good grocery? Where can you get your hair cut? Which doctors accept your insurance? Are there any parks nearby? Yes, Naomi was from Bethlehem, but she'd left over a decade before, and she and Ruth were low on resources. Making this move alone would have been brutal. But having a godly friend to process it all with made everything easier. I would have loved to have heard some of these ladies' conversations—the discussions about where to live and whom to trust and what their priorities should be. I would have loved to have witnessed their laughter, tears, hugs, and prayers. Amy and I feel we have more hope, strength, and courage because we have each other. Ruth and Naomi must have felt the same way.

One thing they needed was food. So Ruth went to a field and spent the day gathering grain. She brought some back to Naomi. Would Naomi have starved without it? We don't know, but maybe.

Another thing they needed was a reputable man to take responsibility for them. It sounds archaic and patriarchal, but this was thousands of years ago in a society where men were the ones who owned land and had money. Without a male protector (usually someone in their family) women were typically homeless, subject to sexual abuse, and often died of starvation.[2] When Naomi heard that Ruth had met Boaz while gathering the grain, the wheels in Naomi's brain started turning.

"Oh, that guy! Wait! I know him. He's actually a relative. A pretty close one. Boaz is kind, has a good reputation. Plus, there's this law that says the nearest relative of our husbands could marry us and take us in. I'm too old, but you, Ruth . . . what did you think of Boaz?" Wink, wink.

Naomi, who was more knowledgeable about the Mosaic law, explained to Ruth the proper way to suggest this marriage. Ruth, wanting a safe future for both of them, followed Naomi's advice to the letter. Please note this wasn't conniving, manipulating, or super weird to marry your dead husband's third cousin. It was not only normal in their culture for a male relative to marry a widow to keep her out of poverty, but was part of the law God gave Moses as an admirable act to provide for widows. A man who would do this was even given a special title, a kinsman-redeemer, because that man would be redeeming a widow from her plight and changing her trajectory. The relative of the deceased husband didn't *have* to marry the widow, but it was a noble thing to do.

The plan worked. Boaz married Ruth and took both Ruth and Naomi into his home. Ruth got pregnant and was able to continue the family name and line that would turn out to be a branch on Jesus's family tree. Boaz became kinsman-redeemer to both Ruth and Naomi. A kinsman-redeemer is as powerful and life-changing as it sounds. Jesus is our Kinsman-Redeemer, saving us from the messy, uncertain lives we would have without Him and inviting us into the protection and love of His amazing grace.

The book of Ruth ends with Grandma Naomi snuggling Ruth and Boaz's son, Obed.

> Naomi took the baby and held him in her arms, cuddling him, cooing over him, waiting on him hand and foot. (4:16 MSG)

And the camera pans out with gentle acoustic guitar music in the background.

We need friends. Christian friends. I didn't always buy into this. I grew up doing my faith on my own. I read my Bible, prayed, and went to church on Sundays. And for the rest of my time? I had a group of friends who barely, if ever, talked about Jesus. I wasn't seeking a Christian friend or Christian community, because I didn't see why they mattered to my day-to-day life.

But I had no idea what I was missing.

When you're anxious and frightened in a challenging and uncertain situation, a Christian friend can remind you that Jesus tells us to be anxious about nothing (Matthew 6:34), to cast our cares on Him (1 Peter 5:7), and to not be afraid but courageous, that we can do all of that because God is with us (Deuteronomy 31:6) and He is for us and helping us fight our battles. And because that's all easier said than done, Christian friends can also pray for and with you.

Having Amy as a friend means I can talk with someone who is balancing similar responsibilities and knows we're supposed to trust God with our time and our talent. We remind each other that God isn't keeping score of how many hours we spend cheering on our kids at their activities or writing chapters but is pleased that we love our kiddos and do the work He created us to do. Have either Amy or I perfectly balanced our roles? No. But we offer each other grace and pep talks and prayers and truth along the way that keep us sane and motivated and focused on Jesus, that keep us from piling unwarranted guilt or self-doubt or comparisons upon ourselves.

I know how God is working in my life, but with Amy I also get to see the prayers God answers in her life, the opportunities and encouragement the Lord gives her, the ways He is faithful to her. Our friendship has expanded my view of God and opened my limited mind to even broader ways the Holy Spirit is on the move.

I would have given up writing if it hadn't been for Amy. It's a tough game filled with relentless rejections—for goodness' sake, J. K. Rowling got twelve rejections before she got an offer for the first Harry Potter book. Those rejections feel personal, make a writer feel like she can't or shouldn't write. Amy would say to me over and over, "The world needs this book," or "Women need to hear your words." And when the days were dark and my heart was heavy, I kept writing because Amy, a seasoned author and editor, kept reminding me of God's faithfulness and His calling on my life. Amy has walked with me as I've journeyed through life just like Ruth stood by Naomi.

You can do life alone.

But it's not how God intended it.

It might feel fine, but it will be missing multiple facets of God's glory and grace. If you try to navigate work, relationships, and faith on your own, you'll limit yourself. God uses friendships to build our faith and empower us further. Moses relied on his brother, Aaron, to speak to Pharaoh. King David relied on his best friend, Jonathan, to keep him safe from King Saul's plans to destroy him. Jesus surrounded Himself with the disciples during His three years of ministry. The apostle Paul thanked many friends in his letters for their support and love that kept him going. And the author of Hebrews gave us this directive:

> And let us consider how we may spur one another on toward love and good deeds, not giving up meeting together, as some are in the habit of doing, but encouraging one another—and all the more as you see the Day approaching. (10:24–25)

Without Ruth, Naomi might not have survived the trip to Bethlehem, had enough food to sustain her, or had a home or a family. Without Naomi, Ruth might have stayed where she was, mourning her husband in a dark room of her father's house, lonely and sad. They could have experienced suffering alone. But that wasn't the plan for either of them. Through the love, support, and loyalty of friendship, our mighty God empowered Ruth and Naomi to bravely start over, to live rich, full lives. Yes, safe and provided for, but also surrounded with love and joy. They were better together. Better on the hard days and the good days, stronger in their struggles and their triumphs.

> If you try to navigate work, relationships, and faith on your own, you'll limit yourself. God uses friendships to build our faith and empower us further.

That's how Amy and I are too. Better together. Stronger together. Braver together. I've listed so many ways she's been here for me over the years in this chapter, but when I emailed Amy asking her permission to write about our friendship and use her name, she said, "I can't wait to read that chapter. You are my Ruth."

"No, you're my Ruth," I answered.

For the record, we decided we could just be Ruth One and Ruth Two.

Friends are a dime a dozen. But true, loyal ones, ones like Amy and Ruth, are few and far between. So how do you find a Ruth in your life?

Don't worry, God wants you to have this kind of friendship. If you ask Him, He will empower you to meet the right people.

Ask God to bring someone to mind. Someone genuine and kind, a good listener who gives advice centered on biblical truth. Reach out to her. Ask if she'll go on a walk or grab a cup of coffee or meet you at the playground so you can chat while your kids pretend they're pirates. It's fantastic to have friends who aren't Jesus followers, but the kind of friend I'm specifically talking about here is the kind that will keep pointing you back to Jesus, His love, and His promises.

Don't know anyone like this? You could sign up for a local Bible study or Christian moms' group like MomCo, or volunteer at the local food pantry or shelter. Are your days already so jammed you can't imagine trying to fit another thing into your schedule? Look around where you already are. Ask God to open your eyes and empower you to see the right person and to bravely step into conversations with them. Does someone you know wear a cross necklace or drink from a coffee mug with a Bible verse on it? Is anyone reading a Christian book or talking about their church? You could sit at their table and strike up a conversation. Stand near them on the sidelines. Linger after work or class or volunteering and ask what she thought about the instructor or seminar that day and go from there.

Some of you are reading this and getting excited about the prospect of finding new friends. You love people and are eager to meet more and have all the conversations.

I, on the other hand, am an introvert and tempted to stay at home instead of "meeting together." But attending the women's Bible study I'm in or going on a walk with my friend Shena or chatting on the phone with Amy never fails to empower me, stir me up in all the right ways, and ignite my trust in God and my passion to shine His light. Engaging with other Christian women sometimes pulls me out of my comfort zone but always makes my life richer.

As Amy said to me in our email exchange after that first shared coffee at Panera, *God knows when we find each other, we find strength, comfort, and wisdom to better do His work.*

Strength.

Comfort.

Wisdom.

Better able to do God's work.

Don't you want that?

God gave that to Ruth and Naomi. He gave it to me and Amy. He wants it for you too.

Forge Friendships

And let us consider how we may spur one another on toward love and good deeds, not giving up meeting together, as some are in the habit of doing, but encouraging one another— and all the more as you see the Day approaching. (Hebrews 10:24–25)

- Do you have a Ruth kind of friend?

    If so, reach out to her today. You could send her a card thanking her for her friendship, snip some flowers from your yard, tie a ribbon around the stems, and drop them by her house, or take her out for her favorite treat.

    If not, reach out to someone in one of the social spheres you're already in (neighborhood, work, book club, volunteer, etc.), or register for a group where you could meet someone new.

11

Go from Bitter to Sweet

Naomi

Every time I talk to my mom, she says, "Laura, I am so blessed!" And she is.

But fifteen years ago, she wouldn't have said that, because she certainly didn't feel that way.

Fifteen years ago, Mom and Dad got divorced after being married for forty-three years. They went on their first date to a junior high dance when they were thirteen and got married their senior year of college. They grew up together. Then all their future plans came crashing down—playing with grandkids, spending time in the mountain vacation home they'd just built together, the football games they had season tickets to, the places they'd dreamed of traveling to, Sunday mornings at church, Saturday morning errands, weeknight dinners, all of it.

It was not at all how my mom expected things to look. She didn't feel blessed. She was devastated. She put her house on the market in an attempt to move on. But due to a number of unforeseen circumstances, Mom was surrounded by memories that hurt her heart for two years

79

before someone bought the house she and Dad had lived in together. Two years of tears and loneliness and not understanding God's plan for her. Two years of offers that fell through, house maintenance she felt overwhelmed by, accounts and policies that had to be transferred out of their names and into hers or his, and two years of desperate prayers lifted up for healing, strength, endurance, hope, and new life.

Have you ever felt this way?

Maybe you feel this way right now. At a dead end. Like the rug got yanked out from under you. Like everything you thought was supposed to happen isn't happening. Maybe you're even wondering if God still sees you, if He's still good and loving or in control.

Mom was worn thin emotionally from the divorce and from losing her husband and partner in life, and physically from trying to get her hot water heater fixed and the gutters cleaned and keeping her house spotless every single day in case a potential buyer came through. And then she found a condo she adored at a price that made sense, and her house sold all in one fell swoop. She not only moved into a gorgeous condo where she didn't have to mow or shovel but was dropped into a neighborhood with a group of people who became *her* people. These neighbors have become her squad. Her besties for the resties. They go on morning walks, have patio hops, and meet at the pool on Wednesday afternoons. They gather in each other's family rooms to do Pilates or watch football. They have each other over for dinner, walk each other's dogs, fix each other's garbage disposals, share recipes, books, stories, and prayers. My mom is surrounded by people who adore her and who she loves right back. She is not lonely. She is full of love. She doesn't wish for her old life back. She is literally living her best life now.

Mom speaks of God's faithfulness, how He was with her always, even during those dark years full of sorrow. She can see God's guidance when she put an offer on a different condo and didn't get it. If she'd moved there, she would never have met some of her favorite people on the planet. She sees God's love even in the divorce. Yes, the divorce was traumatic, but the marriage was causing her trauma. Trauma she's now healing from. God stood beside Mom, allowing her to lean into His might when she didn't have enough on her own. God led her through some tough terrain and out the other side. Today Mom laughs louder, lives more freely, and after years of being gaslighted, is embracing the awesome giving, loving person she was created to be, braver and stronger than ever.

A woman named Naomi (remember her from the last chapter?) also found herself in a situation she never imagined—with the future she'd dreamed of crashing down around her. She, her husband, and their two sons had to move because there was a famine where they lived. In their new land Naomi's husband, Elimelech, died. I'm guessing she was heartbroken, but she still had her boys, who both married local women, and the five of them lived happily together for ten years.

Then the unthinkable happened. *Both* Naomi's sons died. Any mama's heart would be devastated, but in her ancient Near Eastern culture this had so many additional implications. Not only did Naomi lose her boys, but she lost the people who were providing for and protecting her. Now Naomi and her two daughters-in-law were left without a provider or protector. Women didn't inherit their husbands' resources, so they were unfortunately dependent on men. Things were bleak. Naomi decided her only option was to return to her homeland in hopes someone would have pity on her and take her in. One of her daughters-in-law, Ruth, swore to stay by Naomi's side. Together they traveled back to Naomi's birthplace of Bethlehem.

I know some of that was repetitive, and it's a lot of background. But it's important.

So far, Naomi has been married, had two sons, experienced famine, relocated, widowed, had her sons die, and is now back in her hometown with one of her daughters-in-law, trying not to drown in desperation. When Naomi and Ruth arrived in Bethlehem and some of the townspeople recognized her. They said,

"Can this be Naomi?"

"Don't call me Naomi," she told them. "Call me Mara [meaning 'bitter'], because the Almighty has made my life very bitter. I went away full, but the LORD has brought me back empty. Why call me Naomi? The LORD has afflicted me; the Almighty has brought misfortune upon me." (Ruth 1:19–21)

Naomi felt bitter, but our mighty God gave her the hope and courage she needed to be brave enough to make that move to Bethlehem because He had goodness waiting for her there.

Do you feel bitter today? Do you feel empty? Perhaps that the Lord has afflicted you? Are you crying out like Naomi?

Even if you feel like you're out of options, our mighty God's possibilities are endless. He will give you the courage you need to take one more step. And then another after that.

That wasn't the end of Naomi's story, and it's not the end of yours either.

He will give you the courage you need to take one more step. And then another after that.

Once in Bethlehem, God did a super cool thing. He introduced one of Naomi's relatives, Boaz, to Naomi's daughter-in-law Ruth *and* had them realize how they were related. Boaz heard how Ruth and Naomi were homeless, jobless, husband- and fatherless, and God prompted Boaz to help. Because of her knowledge of Jewish law, Naomi saw the opportunity and came up with a plan. She coached Ruth how to let Boaz know she was interested in accepting his support. There were some complicated rules, traditions, and laws in place, but Boaz

1. bought a piece of land that apparently still belonged to Naomi's deceased husband, providing an unexpected healthy retirement fund for Naomi; and
2. married Ruth.

Voilà! Naomi and Ruth were provided for, and Boaz would protect them both. Ruth got pregnant and had a son. They named their baby boy Obed.

This is God's way of tying everything together with a neat bow. The family line that fizzled out when Naomi's boys died was saved by Obed, who would carry the family name (remember Boaz was a relative of Naomi's husband). Obed would also one day be King David's grandpa. Wowza—as in *the* King David. Yup. Who knew? Oh, God did. Only He could orchestrate such intricate details. God saw Naomi, who lost her entire immediate family and was penniless. He saved her and her story.

Don't take it from me. Take it from the women in Bethlehem who witnessed the whole thing. They said to Naomi,

> "Praise be to the LORD, who this day has not left you without a guardian-redeemer. May [the baby, Obed] become famous throughout Israel! He will renew your life and sustain you in your old age. For your daughter-in-law, who loves you and who is better to you than seven sons, has given him birth."
> Then Naomi took the child in her arms and cared for him. The women living there said, "Naomi has a son!" And they named him Obed. He was the father of Jesse, the father of David. (Ruth 4:14–17)

Our mighty God's intervention in Naomi's life took her from hopeless to full of hope for a future. From ready to give up to brave enough to orchestrate a plan for Ruth to marry Boaz. If you would have asked Naomi, she would have told you she was no longer bitter. She would have echoed my mom's words: "I am so blessed!"

Despite her tragedies, despite her life not being at all how she expected it, God never left Naomi. Naomi couldn't see it when her husband or sons died, but God was there. God arranged for Naomi's son to marry Ruth, a woman who would faithfully stay by Naomi's side. God escorted and empowered Ruth and Naomi, two vulnerable women, safely through a rugged journey of approximately fifty miles on foot.[1] God took care of all the details of legalities and property rights and family law so Boaz could marry Ruth. God gave Ruth a son, even though she hadn't been able to get pregnant for the ten years she was married to Naomi's son. God provided redemption for Naomi: a new life, a grandson to cuddle, a home to live in, and a family—albeit different from the one she imagined—of Ruth, Boaz, and Obed to grow old with. Wow! That's a heck of a lot of pieces God put into place. No wonder it took a while.

Is there part of your life right now that feels like it's disintegrating? Like you thought it would go one way, but it's gone a totally different direction? Do you feel bitter? Did someone leave? Is there an addiction? A loss? Did the rules all change?

Take a deep breath.

I have no idea how you're going to get from here to there—but God does. He will empower you. He's still good. He still loves you. You can put your hope in Him.

God arranged a new chapter in Naomi's story she could have never written for herself. But God didn't just do this in the Bible. He did it for my mom.

The two-year waiting period of not selling her house, mourning her marriage, being so full of sadness that it spilled out in buckets of tears, and the reality of not knowing what was next was brutal for my sweet mama. She didn't understand why she had been dealt the hand she was holding. Would she ever feel loved again? Would she feel this lonely for the rest of her life? Why was it taking so long to sell her house?

But God was moving all the pieces into place. Setting up the perfect buyer for her home. Waiting until just the right condo was available. Even moving two other couples into her new neighborhood, so when she got there, beautiful friendships could blossom. God was also gifting Mom with priceless moments with her grandchildren, reminding her how adored she was, giving her hope through her time in prayer and Bible reading, and making her brave enough to keep moving forward even on what felt like the most bitter days. Our mighty God never stops working. We can put our hope in Him.

I don't know where you feel bitter or sad today. But I know that

God sees you and He's working on making your life sweet again. He's gathering the ingredients, letting something come to room temperature in one bowl, allowing the butter to soften in another, and roasting another ingredient in the oven. He's lining everything up and stirring it together. Sometimes it takes time, sometimes longer than we'd like. Often the sweet stage isn't at all how we hoped or planned. There could still be pain and loss along the way. But God loves you and wants the best for you. He'll empower you to find sweetness again.

What does that look like? I don't know. But when God has everything prepared, you'll be able to confidently proclaim, "I am blessed. I am no longer bitter. In fact, my life is pretty sweet."

Go from Bitter to Sweet

He will renew your life and sustain you. (Ruth 4:15)

• Are you struggling with sorrow or pain like Naomi did? Is there a part of your story (or in the story of someone you love) that looks bleak?

Try incorporating the hymn "My Hope Is Built on Nothing Less" by Edward Mote into your prayer time this week:

> My hope is built on nothing less
> than Jesus' blood and righteousness
> I dare not trust the sweetest frame
> but wholly lean on Jesus' name.
> When darkness veils His lovely face,
> I rest on His unchanging grace.
> In every high and stormy gale.
> My anchor holds within the veil.
> On Christ the solid Rock I stand
> All other ground is sinking sand
> All other ground is sinking sand.[2]

Write it out. Pray it out loud. Google it, play it, and let the lyrics wash over you. Sing it out loud if you like. God wants to hear your hurts and fears. And He also wants you to put your hope in Him. It is in Him that you will find joy and peace, that your life will be made sweet.

12

Pour Your Heart Out

Hannah

If you want to chat with the CEO of an organization, you can't just show up at his or her office. You have to schedule a meeting. And those are hard to come by. You'll probably be delegated to a vice president of this or that and not actually reach the CEO. If you want to share an idea with the president of the United States, you'll have to go through your local senator or representative, and you'll most likely interact with one of their interns, not your congressperson directly. If you want to tell Oprah something, good luck even finding a phone number or email where you could attempt to reach her. Her website won't even allow you to suggest a book title for her book club. This is nothing against any of these in-fluential people. They have a limited number of hours in their days (just like us) but thousands of people who want their time (maybe less like us).

Jesus has even more people wanting to tell Him something, ask Him something, complain to Him about something, beg Him for something, share something with Him, thank Him—and yet He makes time for all of us. And not just a fifteen-minute slot four Thursdays from today but anytime, anywhere, right now, right where you are. The Lord will give you His full attention and take the time to listen about anything and everything you want to discuss.

A woman named Hannah believed this. Her husband, Elkanah, had two wives, Hannah and Peninnah. First Samuel 1:2 tells us, "Peninnah had children, but Hannah had none." Which stinks if you're Hannah and want to have kids, but that pain is escalated by the fact that their society valued women for their ability to produce heirs. And just to make the whole your-husband-has-another-wife-and-she-has-kids-and-you-don't situation worse, Peninnah frequently made fun of Hannah for not having kids. *Ouch.* This situation seemed to especially flare up on their family's annual trip to the tabernacle to worship and sacrifice to the Lord. On one of these trips, when Peninnah was taunting Hannah as usual (that would be so great to live with), Hannah got up and went to pray.

> Hannah stood up. Now Eli the priest was sitting on his chair by the doorpost of the LORD's house. In her deep anguish Hannah prayed to the LORD, weeping bitterly. And she made a vow, saying, "LORD Almighty, if you will only look on your servant's misery and remember me, and not forget your servant but give her a son, then I will give him to the LORD for all the days of his life, and no razor will ever be used on his head."
>
> As she kept on praying to the LORD, Eli observed her mouth. Hannah was praying in her heart, and her lips were moving but her voice was not heard. Eli thought she was drunk and said to her, "How long are you going to stay drunk? Put away your wine."
>
> "Not so, my lord," Hannah replied, "I am a woman who is deeply troubled. I have not been drinking wine or beer; I was pouring out my soul to the LORD." (1 Samuel 1:9–15)

When was the last time you poured out your heart to the Lord? That you prayed so fervently someone might have mistaken you for drunk? That you stepped away from the situation that triggered or taunted or terrified you and lost yourself in prayer? Not just telling a troubled friend in a text, *I'm praying for you*, or silently saying, *Jesus, please be with me,* or closing your eyes during church and letting the words of the pastor's prayer wash over you. All of those are good things—sending encouraging texts to friends, whispering quick prayers throughout the day, receiving lovely prayers prayed over us. But there is a difference between this kind of prayer and an all-out praying while you stomp around your house, angry at a situation, or collapse on the couch or floor and pray through tears, maybe not even words, but mumblings and emotions pouring out of you. Or praying for the same thing for three days or months or years or decades and faithfully returning to that prayer over and over again.

Do you pour your heart out to the Lord?

Because God invites us to.

And when we pour our hearts out to the Lord, it changes us.

After praying, Hannah still didn't know the outcome; a child didn't miraculously drop into her lap. She wasn't instantly pregnant. The Bible doesn't say that Peninnah was transformed into a kind and supportive friend. Sure, Eli told her, "May God answer your prayer." Which probably felt reassuring, but *God* didn't tell Hannah He would answer her prayer. Still, immediately Hannah was better. She "went back and began to eat again, and she was no longer sad" (verse 18 NLT). Not because Hannah got what she wanted, but because talking with God helps. He's the very best listener. He helps direct our thoughts. He comforts us. He centers us. He reminds us of what is truly important. He reassures us that He loves us and wants good for us. And that is a soothing balm for our cracked and dry souls.

What's holding us back from praying all out like this? From pouring our hearts out in prayer?

Is it okay if we also pray quietly, silently in our heads, pray Scripture or rote prayers, write our prayers in a journal? Yes! All of these work. Jesus simply wants us to talk to Him. That's the goal of prayer—spending time with the One who loves us most and best.

Jesus tells us,

> Ask and it will be given to you; seek and you will find; knock and the door will be opened to you. For everyone who asks

receives; the one who seeks finds; and to the one who knocks,
the door will be opened. (Matthew 7:7–8)

Jesus doesn't say we need fancy words or that we need to have training in prayer. He doesn't require us to pray at a certain time or place.
He doesn't say we can only ask for the needs of others or that we have
to keep our composure. No. Jesus says we can go straight to God,
march right into the home of the CEO of the universe, and ask for our
daily needs, forgiveness, discernment, peace, hope, love, a fresh start,
protection, you name it. And when we ask Him? We'll receive. When
we seek answers or hope or strength or courage or energy? We'll find
them. But we have to knock.

What's restraining us from praying for all the things? From knocking and seeking and asking?

Hannah had this right! She was upset—and she started knocking
on God's door. We don't have to hold back or keep it together. Jesus
is the safe place where we can pound our fists, weep like a baby, look
plain crazy, or even, like Hannah, appear drunk. You have passions in
your heart. You have things you're terrified of. You have something so
personal you're not sure who you could even share it with. You have
big dreams and things that might seem trivial to others but matter so
much to you in this moment now. Take them to Jesus! He's all ears!

When I was nursing our third baby, I had a clogged milk duct. If
you've had one you know how painful that is. Each time your baby
takes a drink, it feels like razor blades are being scraped inside your
breast. And yet you want to feed your baby because she's hungry and
can't feed herself. I remember sitting in a chair, holding my baby girl,
tears of pain streaming down my face. I felt so helpless. I just started
praying, "Jesus, please make this better. Please unclog this duct. Please
help me be able to feed my baby. I'm so grateful for her. I'm so in awe
of the fact that You created my body to produce milk to feed her. It's
truly miraculous. *Ow!* But, Lord, please help."

I doubt if my thoughts were that articulate through the pain, but
that's what I kept circling back to—amazement at how God designed
the human body, *pain*, begging for healing, *pain*, a sense of aloneness,

pain, and responsibility to sustain my tiny girl. My two other kiddos were five and two-and-a-half years old. My husband, though sweet, had no clue what to do. My mom bottle-fed me and my brother and had zero experience in this arena. And here I sat hurting and crying while holding my baby. But as I prayed, I felt God's presence with me. I got through that feeding. My little girl was full, snuggly, and smiley. I got a break from the pain. God assured me He would heal me. He hadn't yet, but He let me know He was there with me. And it was calming. For each subsequent feeding I prayed my way through it. The pain was fierce but bearable. The next afternoon the duct unclogged— such sweet relief. The next day may be speedy for a prayer to be an- swered, but that was seven painful feedings later. I fully believe my continued prayer for something as tiny as a single milk duct changed the entire scenario. Through prayer, God emboldened me and calmed me—not because the prayer was instantly answered but because I was reassured that God was with me and helping me, and that was a game changer.

When we knock, He answers. When we seek, we find. When we go to God, God rearranges our thoughts and renews our minds.

> Do not conform to the pattern of this world, but be trans- formed by the renewing of your mind. Then you will be able to test and approve what God's will is—his good, pleasing and perfect will. (Romans 12:2)

This is the key: not letting ourselves think like the world does, but instead asking, seeking, knocking like Hannah did. Taking our thoughts to Jesus and asking Him to help us sort through them. When we do, He shows us good things. Pleasing outcomes. Paths forward. For Hannah, in her patriarchal culture where having sons was where a woman's worldly value lay, she could have bought into the lie that without kids she was worthless. Hannah could have fallen for Penin- nah's taunting and believed that "the LORD had kept her from having children" (1 Samuel 1:6 NLT). But instead, Hannah said no to what culture said. She removed herself from the noise of the world—ahem,

Peninnah mocking her—walked away, found a place to pray, and poured her heart out to God, letting Him transform her thinking to what was possible.

When we knock, He answers.
When we seek, we find.

This is what prayer does.

God uses it to empower you too.

The darkness might not immediately turn to light. The cancer might not vanish. The confrontation might still loom. But when we talk to Jesus, we feel a bit better. It reframes our thoughts from *I'm doomed!* to *There's hope.* We are reminded that our Lord sees us and hasn't forgotten us. Prayer makes us brave because, when we talk to God, He reminds us He is loving and good and mighty and in control. Talking to Jesus changes things because He is a comforter, friend, advocate, healer, creator, the Prince of Peace, the Great I Am, the Savior of the world, the beginning and the end.

We could leave off here: Prayer changes things.

That feels like a great punctuation mark on the topic. But what we do when a prayer is answered is also important to discuss. Because so often I know what I do. I think, *Oh wow! My duct is cleared. Thanks, God.* And move on. But wait! The God of the universe just let me walk straight up to Him, share my secrets and worries, and ask for my desires to come true, and He granted my wish? And all I did was mumble a thanks?

We can learn from Hannah in this department too.

God answered Hannah's prayer. She got pregnant, had a son, and named him Samuel, which comes from the Hebrew term for "heard by God." Once Samuel was weaned, in a harrowing act of obedience, Hannah took him to the tabernacle in Shiloh (where she'd poured out her heart in prayer) to keep her promise—that if God would give her a son, she would give that son to the Lord to serve Him.

Then Hannah prayed:

"My heart rejoices in the LORD!
  The LORD has made me strong.
Now I have an answer for my enemies;
  I rejoice because you rescued me.
No one is holy like the LORD!
  There is no one besides you;
  there is no Rock like our God.

". . . For all the earth is the LORD's,
  and he has set the world in order."
      (1 Samuel 2:1–2, 8 NLT)

Hannah didn't just say thanks and move on. She wrote an entire song thanking God for what He did. Touting His goodness, His holiness, that He has set the world in order. She didn't do this praising where no one could hear. She could have, and that would have still been great. But she went the extra mile. Eli the high priest was there. Hannah's son, Samuel, was there. We don't know if her husband and his other wife were present or not. But Hannah declared God's goodness and faithfulness out loud to both the man in charge of shepherding God's people at the time and her own son, whom she loved dearly.

What a gorgeous reminder to you and me. When God answers a prayer, yes, we should thank Him. But also, we should sing His praises to others. We don't have to sing, which is fortunate because I can't carry a tune. But we can tell our pastors and Bible study teachers and mentors so they can be encouraged. They need to see God on the move, just like we do. We can tell our families, "Oh my goodness! I was praying for this, and God answered my prayer!" We can tell our coworker or the friend we walk with, "You know how I was really worried about [fill in the blank]—well, you'll never believe what God did." And proceed to tell them all about it.

And if they think we're crazy or drunk, we know what happened. We know that God is good and heard us and answered our prayers. Plus, we're planting seeds. At a minimum, somewhere in the back of that person's mind they'll be processing, *Wait, Laura asked God for that thing and then it happened? Hmm.* We are sharing with them the power of prayer, encouraging and inspiring them to keep praying, keep trusting, to continue bringing their needs and hopes to the Lord. And if they never have before, it might just be the impetus that person needs to start! Plus, sharing with others also cements the truth of God's goodness in our hearts, helping us remember what He did for us.

So what is your heart's desire today? Not that you'll win the lottery or become the next Avenger, but really and truly, where are you broken and need mending, downcast and need lifting, stuck and need jump-starting? Pour your heart out to your loving Father. He's listening. And simply spending time with Him will always strengthen, empower, and calm your soul.

Pour Your Heart Out

Ask and it will be given to you; seek and you will find; knock and the door will be opened to you. For everyone who asks receives; the one who seeks finds; and to the one who knocks, the door will be opened. (Matthew 7:7–8)

- Start praying for that thing, your heart's desire, today. Like Hannah, don't delay—just take your concerns to God and pour your heart out.
- Consider starting a prayer journal and write out your prayers or simply list the things you talked to Jesus about. When prayers are answered, go back and highlight or mark them. It's powerful and empowering to look back and see how many prayers God answered.

- You could also designate a specific time each day you'll pray for your need. When you first wake up. While you're on your morning drive. On your lunch break. Anytime works. Keep praying.

13

Act Quickly

Abigail

Six passports were in the bedazzled black backpack I'd gotten during my study abroad trip to London. Our suitcases were lined up in the hallway at the top of the stairs. The cab would be arriving in thirty-five minutes. My husband was teaching a monthlong class in Ecuador, and the kids and I were going with him. We were excited to explore volcanoes, ancient Inca ruins, and elaborate cathedrals. We wanted to work on rolling our *r*'s and to sample authentic Ecuadorian empanadas that were crisp on the outside and filled with warm, gooey cheese. None of us had ever been to Ecuador, and we were eager for whatever God had in store for us there.

But our youngest had a fever of 102 degrees. Not ideal for traveling to South America. It had started the day before. We'd hoped it would be a twenty-four-hour thing. That a day in bed with some acetaminophen and lots of fluids would do the trick. But he still had a fever when we woke on our travel day. And it was still dangerously high.

"I'm fine," he said in his sweet little seven-year-old voice. "I feel much better. I can go."

But his eyes were glassy and his face flushed.

I could give him more medicine, put him in his coziest clothes, cuddle him on the flight, and hope he would feel better. But what if he didn't? What if he got really sick, and we couldn't bring his fever down and were stuck in an unknown country? I couldn't stay home with our youngest and send Brett ahead with the other three kids. He couldn't juggle all his teaching responsibilities in Ecuador *and* some of our kiddos. But if we didn't go, Brett would have to go alone. We'd be away from him for weeks—longer than we'd ever been away from each other. All the kids would miss out on the adventure our family had gotten so excited about. And we'd already paid for the plane tickets, the accommodations for six. We'd lose so much money. We had very little time to make a big decision. And I don't operate well in those scenarios. I'm not spontaneous. I prefer to plan ahead—and plan thoroughly—then stick to that plan. But like it or not, the clock was ticking, and we had to act quickly.

I'm not the first or last woman to be faced with making an important decision on a tight timeline. Abigail's mind must have also been a tornado of what-if scenarios as she tried to decide what to do. Her situation was extremely serious, and time was of the essence. Her "mean and surly" husband Nabal had disrespected the anointed future king, David, and his giant army of loyal men. David and his men had protected Nabal's shepherds and sheep in the wilderness. Now David and his army needed food and asked Nabal for provision. That might seem a bit forward to us, but in David and Nabal's time, providing for travelers was the social norm. Hospitality was assumed and part of the Jewish law.

Nabal gave a hard pass, saying, "Why should I take my bread and water, and the meat I have slaughtered for my shearers, and give it to men coming from who knows where?" (1 Samuel 25:11).

Nabal knew who David was and where he came from. Nabal's comments were arrogant and untrue. Insulted and furious, David ordered four hundred of his men to "strap on their swords," stating he would kill every male in Nabal's household. That's a lot of guys and a lot of weapons.

Back home, Abigail's shepherds filled her in on the crisis at hand and said, "Now think it over and see what you can do" (verse 17). Her home, family, everything she knew was in danger—all those soldiers and swords were headed her way. Abigail didn't have much time to "think it over"; she had to do something! And quickly.

If Abigail went against her wicked husband, he might divorce her, leaving her disgraced, homeless, and penniless. (Men didn't need much of a reason to divorce their wives those days.) Nabal was the kind of guy who wouldn't think twice about beating or killing her if she went against his will.

But if Abigail did nothing, they'd all be slaughtered.

Divorce, physical harm, family devastation. Abigail had zero good options.

Have you been there? With choices, but no good choices? Where you'll cause ripples, if not waves, no matter what you decide?

The Bible tells us "Abigail acted quickly" (verse 18). She couldn't wallow in the what-ifs but had to move fast. Abigail threw together an impromptu picnic for hundreds of warriors, sent her servants with her gift of food and wine, hopped on her donkey, and followed.

> When Abigail saw David, she quickly got off her donkey and bowed down before David with her face to the ground. She fell at his feet and said: "Pardon your servant, my lord, and let me speak to you; hear what your servant has to say." (verses 23–24)

A woman approaching an anointed king (or any other man) she wasn't married to was an extremely bold move, but Abigail had made up her mind and bravely stuck with it. Abigail begged David to ignore Nabal and his foolishness, and instead accept the gigantic meal she brought. She recognized David was a man of God, saying, "The LORD your God will certainly make a lasting dynasty for my lord, because you fight the LORD's battles, and no wrongdoing will be found in you as long as you live" (verse 28).

David accepted Abigail's offer and canceled the order to kill Nabal's household. Whew! Disaster averted. Not only did Abigail save the lives of everyone in her home, but she also stopped David from committing carnage he might later regret. Despite all the potential consequences, Abigail was able to act quickly based on two criteria:

1. What was true?
2. What was God's will?

Abigail knew Nabal was mean and rude, and David was on the Lord's side. She was familiar with the passages from the Torah that talked about being hospitable to strangers, like "If a stranger dwells with you in your land, you shall not mistreat him. The stranger who dwells among you shall be to you as one born among you, and you shall love him as yourself" (Leviticus 19:33–34 NKJV). I also believe our mighty God nudged Abigail into action, giving her the courage to take David and his troops a meal. Once we're focused on the truth and God's will instead of the distractions and what-ifs, God can help us bravely make wise and timely decisions just like He did for Abigail.

Our family's quick travel decision wasn't nearly as serious as the one Abigail had to make, but that January morning it felt critical that we choose correctly. Brett and I ducked into our closet to chat without four little pairs of ears listening. Our conversation swirled for a few minutes but landed on two questions.

1. What was true?
2. What was God's will?

> Once we're focused on the truth and God's will instead of the distractions and what-ifs, God can help us bravely make wise and timely decisions.

The truth was Brett had a commitment to his employer *and* Maguire was sick and shouldn't travel. Even if we all wanted to go. After a few deep breaths and focusing on the facts, God's will became crystal clear. When the cab arrived at our house, Brett was the only one who got in.

Later in Abigail's story, Nabal died, and David married Abigail. But on the day she learned her husband had refused hospitality to the mighty David, Abigail didn't know that yet. Still Abigail avoided getting tangled up in the hypotheticals. She bravely kept her eyes on the truth and God's will and acted quickly.

I believe Abigail would counsel you and me to do the same. Even if it's uncomfortable or challenging. Even if there are potential downsides. Even if we might be dismissed, unfollowed, or left out. When we keep our eyes on the truth and God's desires for us, we can more clearly see how to respond. Our mighty God will make us brave enough to take the step, call someone out, sign on the line, bow out, raise our hand, send the invitation, bite our tongue, resist temptation, or turn in our resignation.

Discerning God's will for us can free us from our worries and tug-of-war thoughts. We can simply say, "Jesus, I don't know what to do. I don't know what's true. Both choices have downsides (or maybe they both have upsides). Please help me know what to choose."

Obviously, depending on the decision, consequences vary in severity. No matter what you're contemplating, Jesus doesn't want you to worry. He wants you to go to Him. It could be a decision as simple as, *Should I order pizza to save stress and time* or *whip something up in the kitchen to save money?* Or maybe it's a choice with more impact like, *Should I sign the lease for an apartment on the spot because if I don't I'll lose the space,* or *wait and see more options?* If you're a teacher, parent, team leader, boss, or coach, you are probably faced with countless decisions you need to make in the moment every single day that affect the well-being of the people you're responsible for. In all these situations, if we turn to the truth and to God, He will show us how to act quickly, wisely, and bravely.

God aided Abigail in making the best decision for her, her family, her household, and even the king.

God helped Brett and me do the best thing for our family. The next day one of our daughters also came down with a fever. The virus lingered. Our two cuties were listless and feverish for another four or five days. Meanwhile, on the flight to Ecuador, Brett experienced the worst turbulence he'd ever encountered. I'm so grateful our sick kids avoided that unsettling flight and could rest and recover in their own beds instead of a hotel room in a foreign country. Not knowing the outcomes but armed with the truth and God's direction, we'd made the right decision.

Let's clear out the what-ifs and instead focus on what we know for certain. Let's ask Jesus for advice. We don't have to know the full outcome right now. Our mighty God will show us what is true and right and help us discern the very best course of quick action so we can bravely go where He steers us.

Act Quickly

Finally, brothers and sisters, whatever is true, whatever is noble, whatever is right, whatever is pure, whatever is lovely, whatever is admirable—if anything is excellent or praiseworthy—think about such things. (Philippians 4:8)

- Do you need to act quickly on something like Abigail did?

    Take a moment to list out what you know is true about your situation.

    Do any Bible verses pop into your mind while making your list or considering your situation? If so, jot them down too.

    Now take your list to Jesus. Ask Him for direction and guidance so you can know His will. Then ask Him for the courage to follow through and make the right decision in a timely manner.

14

Seek Wisdom

Queen of Sheba

I'm starting something new, and it's not going as quickly as I'd like. Actually, it's not totally new, just a new direction in my ministry, a huge jump start on something I've been doing small for over a decade. God gave me an idea—this growing, expanding, way-bigger vision. He confirmed it in my heart and in my husband's heart too. When I shared this idea with a few trusted friends they all said, "I love this for you." "You are gifted at this." "Yes!" Unprompted, a woman from church shared something with me that totally confirmed I should plant the seeds for this thing and that God would grow it and make it bloom.

So I've taken some initial steps. I've sent out some feeler emails. I've prayed and prayed. And I'm seeking wisdom. I signed up for a class. I hired a coach. Because even though it's something I've been doing, I obviously don't know everything. There are people who have gone before me, who have studied this thing and done it on a larger scale and have knowledge they can share with me. Why wouldn't I ask for their insight?

Well, for one thing, because it's scary to make the ask—to tell people what I'm dreaming about. It's also an investment of time and money for the class and coach, which feels risky. There are no guaranteed outcomes.

An incredible woman in the Bible also sought wisdom. Asking for advice wasn't easy for her either. It was extremely pricey, both monetarily and timewise. She didn't ask for advice because she wasn't smart or didn't have resources. I believe God was after the woman's heart and used wisdom as the vehicle to catch her attention. God will do this for people in our lives too—spark a curiosity that leads them to a church gathering, worship event, or Bible study, or to start asking questions or googling facts. Maybe this is how you came to know Jesus. Maybe God nudged you to want to find out more about Him. There were no guarantees this woman would get the answers she was looking for or even how that wisdom would empower her further. But she knew in her gut it was worth the journey, and so journey she did.

> When the queen of Sheba heard about the fame of Solomon and his relationship to the LORD, she came to test Solomon with hard questions. Arriving at Jerusalem with a very great caravan—with camels carrying spices, large quantities of gold, and precious stones—she came to Solomon and talked with him about all that she had on her mind. Solomon answered all her questions; nothing was too hard for the king to explain to her. When the queen of Sheba saw all the wisdom of Solomon and the palace he had built, the food on his table, the seating of his officials, the attending servants in their robes, his cup-bearers, and the burnt offerings he made at the temple of the LORD, she was overwhelmed. (1 Kings 10:1–5)

The queen of Sheba traveled over fifteen hundred miles from her home country to see Solomon and hear about his relationship with the Lord.

By camel.

It's estimated this trip would have taken seventy-five days each way—two and a half months. That's a heck of a road trip to get some wisdom. And she was already a queen for crying out loud. A wealthy and powerful queen.

The queen of Sheba already knew how to rule a nation, live the life of royalty, and make her kingdom prosperous. So why did she need to seek wisdom? Because the queen of Sheba heard that Solomon was the wisest guy around. To hone her craft—to do her job better—the queen of Sheba realized she could benefit from what Solomon knew. Even after this realization, I'm guessing the Holy Spirit prompted her to go for it—to make the trip and seek Solomon's secret sauce.

What are you in the midst of? Do you know how to do it? Are you trying something new? Expanding your reach? Did you get thrown in blind? Are you upping your game? Aiming for the next level? Do you feel a stirring in your heart to get going, try something new, step up?

Maybe you're a runner who's ready for her first marathon or a professor trying to get tenure or a writer ready to write your next book. Maybe you're a homeowner, but you're moving from the city to the country or from one state to another. Maybe you're going to have a baby, or you already have one but need advice on the transition from one to two. Perhaps you're going for your degree, trying a new medium for your art, or turning your hobby into a business. Or you've participated in dozens of Bible studies but now you're ready to teach one. You could use some wisdom.

Seeking wisdom will most likely cost you something—time, money, pride. You might have to overcome your fear of approaching that mama at the grocery store who seems to be juggling three kids effortlessly. You might have to get the guts to introduce yourself to the person at the meet and greet or send the email or make the call. You might need to sign up for and attend the seminar or devote time to research or take a class or get certified. You might need to hire a babysitter so you can get to where you need to get and meet who you need to meet and focus on the tasks at hand without anybody crawling on your lap or needing to go potty. You might need to travel to that workshop or similar business or expert and pay for airfare, hotel, cab, and admittance. Or maybe you'll need to treat the person whose wisdom you're seeking to a decent dinner or at least a latte. If you feel the Spirit prompting you to go, it's probably time to seek that wisdom.

Some of the things you'll try won't work.

I never got a response from several of the emails I sent out. Some advice I received wasn't as wise as I'd hoped. A few of the class sessions were really for something else altogether, not for what I'm pursuing. Some of my leads seem promising but are taking an incredibly long time. They'd love to meet—six months from now. They're very interested in considering me as part of their plan—for next year. And so it is with new endeavors and seeking wisdom.

Who else had the queen of Sheba sought wisdom from? Had she asked the advice of her parents before she inherited the throne? Had she arranged meetings with neighboring rulers prior to heading to Jerusalem? Did the queen of Sheba feel like it was taking forever fifty days into her journey? Was she underwhelmed when she saw Solomon's palace in the distance (before seeing its splendor up close)? It was lovely and all that, but so was hers. We don't have all the details of the visit, but we do know

1. the queen of Sheba sought Solomon's wisdom,
2. she was willing to travel far and pay greatly for it, and
3. after their time together she said this to the king:

The report I heard in my own country about your achievements and your wisdom is true. But I did not believe what they said until I came and saw with my own eyes. Indeed, not even half the greatness of your wisdom was told me; you have far exceeded the report I heard. How happy your people must be! How happy your officials, who continually stand before you and hear your wisdom! (2 Chronicles 9:5–7)

What did the queen of Sheba do with that wisdom? And was it worth it?

She said the wisdom she gained far exceeded what she expected. All those days on the back of a smelly camel, all the nights sleeping in a makeshift tent instead of her luxurious palace, all the time away from her people was worth it. Because she received great wisdom. I believe the wisdom that most blew her away was the knowledge she gained of our mighty God.

Where's the proof that it was worth it?

1. Right after the queen said how great Solomon's wisdom was, she paid Solomon greatly for it. The text tells us she gave the king "120 talents of gold, large quantities of spices, and precious stones. Never again were so many spices brought in as those the queen of Sheba gave to King Solomon" (1 Kings 10:10). Also, she sent ships filled with gold, cargoes full of precious sandalwood, and more precious stones. The queen would not have given all that wealth to Solomon if she hadn't benefited from the answers he gave her.

2. The stories of this great queen are still being told. She apparently took the wisdom Solomon gave her and applied it, greatly impacting her kingdom and the people who lived there. Both Yemen and Ethiopia still claim this magnificent queen as theirs today. There are fabulous tales about her dynasty and the temple she built. Some say the ark of the covenant (where the Ten Commandments are stored) is hidden in that temple. Others say she had a son with Solomon. What is fact, and what is fiction? I'll let you decide. But her legend lives on over three thousand years later. The wisdom she worked for paid off.

3. Jesus spoke of this great queen and how her wisdom-seeking was something we should learn from.

The Queen of the South will rise at the judgment with this generation and condemn it; for she came from the ends of the earth to listen to Solomon's wisdom, and now something greater than Solomon is here. (Matthew 12:42)

Okay, so even Jesus told us we should pay attention to the queen of Sheba's quest for wisdom.

Are we? Are we learning from her? Putting in the extra effort to find wisdom? Or will we miss the wisdom in front of us because we're too busy or preoccupied or afraid to try, or assume we've got it all figured out? Are we dismissing the promptings of the Spirit? Or leaning in and bravely seeking wisdom?

The queen of Sheba sought wisdom from Solomon out of all the people in the world because Solomon was considered the wisest—he was the expert. Why was he the wisest? Because one night God appeared to Solomon and told this new king He would give him anything he wanted. Solomon asked God for understanding, the ability to discern—wisdom. God was so pleased with Solomon's ask that He granted it, plus so much more.

Aha! Now we're onto something exciting.

The queen of Sheba sought Solomon's wisdom because Solomon had *God's* wisdom. So (1) we can be empowered by other people's wisdom, and (2) the ultimate wisdom comes from our mighty God. Therefore, when we're looking for help or discernment or clarity, we can start by asking King Jesus, who is always with us. He tells us, "But seek first his kingdom and his righteousness, and all these things will be given to you as well" (Matthew 6:33).

How do we tap into Jesus's wisdom?

Reading Matthew, Mark, Luke, and John in the Bible is a great place to start. We can hear the words Jesus spoke and what He had to say about certain subjects. We can also see how Jesus acted and treated others. There is so much wisdom on those pages!

We can also pray. Jesus is available 24/7 for us to talk to. We can ask Him any question, seek first His kingdom. He wants goodness for us. He promises to direct our steps.

Through our Bible reading and prayer time, Jesus will help us figure out where, when, and from whom we should seek wisdom here on earth. We can open our senses to all the ways Jesus provides this wisdom for us. Sometimes it's through the counsel of a wise friend or an expert on YouTube or a speaker at a seminar. Sometimes it's through a class God prompts us to take or a book someone suggests we read. Jesus wants to empower us to do the good work He calls us into. When we seek His wisdom, He'll help us find it in limitless ways.

There's nothing wrong with asking for help. We don't have to act like we know everything or have all the answers. We don't—no matter how long we've been at it.

> Jesus wants to empower us to do the good work He calls us into. When we seek His wisdom, He'll help us find it in limitless ways.

What do you need to know? What are you curious about? What information would help you move forward, take the next step, or get out of a rut? Who has that wisdom? How could you go about contacting them?

Many say that modern Ethiopia's faith in God originated from the queen of Sheba and what she learned during her time with Solomon. Praise God for how He used the queen's journey to bring countless people to Him.

My journey of seeking wisdom led me to resources that helped me fine-tune my strategy and connected me to people whose wisdom I know I will continue to tap into. I learned a lot but feel the Spirit stirring me to keep learning in this area, so I'm still seeking.

Sometimes it will be quite a journey to find wisdom. But our mighty God will be with us on those journeys, empowering us and helping us discover it every step of the way. You'll probably have to do some searching. You'll most likely have to get out of your comfort zone. It could require some sort of investment of time, money, or both on your part. But if you seek Jesus first, He'll make you brave enough to try, and what you learn will be worth more than all the riches of Solomon and the queen of Sheba combined.

Seek Wisdom

But seek first his kingdom and his righteousness, and all these things will be given to you as well. (Matthew 6:33)

- Where could you, like the queen of Sheba, use some wisdom right now? Why?
- Read one chapter of your favorite gospel account each day this week. (Don't have one? I suggest John.) Before you open your Bible, ask Jesus to give you wisdom as you read the words.
- Find a quiet place where you can be alone for fifteen minutes. Close your eyes and ask Jesus for wisdom. Try to keep your mind and heart open and focused on this issue. See if He brings anything to mind.
- Brainstorm five ways you might gain wisdom about this topic. You could grab coffee with someone who is already good at this thing, read a book, sign up for a webinar or workshop, take a class, join a club, ask friends for advice, watch a documentary, listen to a podcast, and so on. Not sure where to start? Google might give you some ideas. Commit this week to trying three of the things you listed.

15

Have Enough
Zarephath's Widow

What do you feel short on? Time? Patience? Food? Money? Sleep? For me, it's usually time.

There are so many things I want to do each day. I want to read books and bake cookies and pray and read my Bible and spend time with my husband and chat with each of my four kids. I want to send cards, messages, and gifts to my friends. I want to go to the farmers' market and listen to a podcast and clean all the bathrooms until their surfaces shine. I want to learn something new and get caught up on my email and write at least three chapters and a blog post. Plus, I have an idea for a whole new book. I want to go for a long run outside and take a hot shower afterward. I'd also like to take a walk with my husband after dinner and paint my nails a fun new color.

There is no human in history who could accomplish all those things in a day. I do realize that, but I still have high aims of what I'll get done. And because I pack my calendar with to-dos and expectations, if someone asks me for more of my time, I often feel tense. I want to give my time to the things *I* scheduled, but of course I would help a friend or neighbor in need, respond to my editor, or call the plumber and be available at the house for his five-hour time window so we can get the toilet fixed, because toilets are important. But it feels like I won't have enough time, like I'll miss doing the important things. And that tangles up my insides. But God always gives me enough time to get the things that truly need done accomplished. And He does so abundantly.

One day I was running around frantically when my husband asked me to read the introduction to a paper he's writing. I thought, *Oh gosh, I want to. I love him. I want to help.* And also, *I don't have the fifteen minutes it will take.* Just then a mom of one of my son's friends texted: *Hey, I can grab the boys after school and run them to rehearsal.*

Wait! What? You can? I thought.

I hadn't even asked for help. And that literally gave me an hour and a half of my day back. So yes, I had time to read my husband's paper. And then some.

Then there was the day I wasn't sure when I'd be able to put together a lesson for the next day's Bible study and one of my kids realized their soccer uniform for that evening's game was dirty. They were stressed with their homework load. I felt like I didn't have enough time to do laundry, but I did it anyway. Because I love my kiddo. And it was the right thing to do. I decided I'd make up Bible study on the fly—for the record, I am not an "on the fly" kind of girl. I'm an INFJ on the Myers-Briggs personality test, if that gives you any insight into the knots in my stomach over trying to spontaneously come up with a lesson. Yet as I simmered veggies for dinner and later drove home from my child's game, God sifted and sorted ideas in my head, filling me with phrases, talking points, and Scripture references so I was completely prepared to teach Bible study.

God is a God of abundance. In little ways like this and in gigantic ways too. We don't have to hold tightly to our resources or fear that we won't have enough. God has more than enough. And He wants to share it with us.

Do I have days that I don't get to everything on my list? When the bed isn't made and dinner isn't cooked and the mail sits unopened? Of course. But here's the thing: I didn't vacuum? No one in my home will notice. I didn't drop off the donations at Goodwill? They're open tomorrow. And the day after that. My nails are chipped and driving me crazy? I'm the only one who cares. I didn't grab those items at the grocery? My kids will survive another day without granola, cheese crackers, and bananas. But the things that really needed to get done did—and sometimes that was taking a nap if I was exhausted or having a long chat with someone I love. I find the things God wants done always get done.

> We don't have to hold tightly to our resources. God has more than enough. And He wants to share it with us.

He is a provider.

There was a woman in the Bible who didn't feel like she had enough. I don't know how she felt about time, but she was short on food and wasn't going to survive if some groceries didn't magically turn up. There was a famine when the Lord told Elijah to go into a village and find a widow who would feed him.

> So [Elijah] went to Zarephath. When he came to the town gate, a widow was there gathering sticks. He called to her and asked, "Would you bring me a little water in a jar so I may have a drink?" As she was going to get it, he called, "And bring me, please, a piece of bread."
>
> "As surely as the LORD your God lives," she replied, "I don't have any bread—only a handful of flour in a jar and a little olive oil in a jug. I am gathering a few sticks to take home and make a meal for myself and my son, that we may eat it—and die." (1 Kings 17:10–12)

The widow didn't have any bread. Not even one of those end pieces nobody wants. She was planning the very last meal for her and her son. I can't imagine. Yes, some days my fridge feels empty. But it's never been *empty* empty. We might not have the ingredients for a favorite meal, but we always have something in the house—a box of pasta, a can of tomatoes, a frozen pizza. I'm blessed that I have never looked at an empty pantry and then to the eyes of my sweet family and thought, *Well, I guess that's it. We're going to starve.*

But that's where this woman was. Her husband was dead. There was a famine in the land, and there was simply nothing to eat. Then a stranger came into town asking *her* for food? She was too weak and exhausted to make a snarky comment or shake her head. Instead, the widow simply stated the facts. And God gave Elijah a message to share with her:

> Don't be afraid. Go home and do as you have said. But first make a small loaf of bread for me from what you have and bring it to me, and then make something for yourself and your son. For this is what the LORD, the God of Israel, says: "The jar of flour will not be used up and the jug of oil will not run dry until the day the LORD sends rain on the land." (1 Kings 17:13–14)

The widow did as Elijah told her.

Even though this was her very last meal, the widow bravely trusted the mighty Lord to provide for her even when she couldn't see His provision.

And . . . the jar of flour was bottomless. It never ran out. The jug of oil was the same—limitless. The woman didn't have to use it sparingly—not that day or the next or the one after that. God provided an abundance of ingredients. Not forever, but until the famine ended. For as long as the widow needed it. Just as He promised. God is a God of abundance, and He always gives us what we need.

What is it you don't have enough of? Boldness? Focus? Energy? Assurance? Ideas?

Careful now. This isn't necessarily what you *want* but what you *need.* There are things we want that aren't the best for us—like my kids wanting four cookies or wanting to stay up late when they were little.

They certainly didn't *need* more sugar or less sleep, but they *wanted* those things. I want things that aren't necessary too—like that adorable sweater I saw in the shop window uptown. So cute. I really want it. But I don't need it.

There are also things we need. They're different. God always gives us what we need. You can count on it. What is it you *need*? God can and will provide it. In abundance. He's a good Father who only wants good things for His kids. How can I be so sure? Because the Bible says so on repeat.

> He who did not spare his own Son, but gave him up for us all—how will he not also, along with him, graciously give us all things? (Romans 8:32)

> The Lord is my shepherd;
>   I have all that I need.
>   (Psalm 23:1 NLT)

> So Abraham called that place The Lord Will Provide. (Genesis 22:14)

We also see God providing in two different instances when Jesus took a couple of fish and a bit of bread and fed thousands and thousands of people (the feeding of the five thousand men in Matthew 14 and the four thousand men in Matthew 15. Note that exponentially more people were fed when you include all the women and children in those crowds). In both miracles, everybody there had more than enough food to fill their bellies. They'd been sitting there all day in one instance (and three days in the other) and felt a little lightheaded, their stomachs began to growl, and they probably whispered to one another, "Does anyone have anything to eat?" "Do you know how far it is to the closest town to get some food?" "Aren't you hungry?" This is when Jesus gathered up what looked like only enough for one person's lunch and turned it into more than an enormous crowd could consume.

I marvel at God's goodness. How abundantly He loves us. How faithfully He provides for us. But still, I have days when I stress out about not having "enough" time or experience or clout or wisdom.

You?

What is it you don't think you have enough of? Are you like the widow, saying, "I don't have any; I think I'm going to die"?

Can I ask the obvious? The thing I need to remind myself. Have you asked God about it? Have you asked Him to give you what you need?

Because God loves you and wants to provide for you abundantly. Just like He loved that widow and gave her not just enough food for herself, but all the food she needed *plus* enough for her son and her unexpected houseguest, Elijah. Just like Jesus loved those thousands of people on a hillside who came to hear Him preach and didn't just turn some fish and bread into enough to tide them over for a little bit, but created such an abundance of food that there were baskets of leftovers the disciples collected afterward. Yup. God loves you and will provide you with everything you need and then some.

God saw that widow in her hunger, and He sees you. God can make a ride from another helpful mom appear out of nowhere for one of your kids, an idea pop into your head for a lesson, a jar of grain inexplicably never run out, or a couple of pieces of bread become meals for thousands.

Sometimes the bank account will still be empty, but the weather is so lovely you can turn off your heater or air conditioner, minimizing your fuel bills. There might be a time when your doctor can't seem to find what's wrong, but God's inexplicable peace floods you. Some days you could feel hopeless or stuck. And at that moment, the kindest text comes from a friend you haven't heard from in ages, reminding you that God sees you and you're not alone. That text seemingly sent by God gives you the hope and courage to continue.

You will have enough. Not because you're great at time or money management, or because you hoarded the supplies or made all the right decisions, but because our mighty God will empower you to have enough, simply by providing it for you. The jar of flour will not be used up and the jug of oil will not run dry. He is the God who can supply what you need today and tomorrow and all the days to come. He will do it abundantly. Not because He has to, but because He loves you.

Have Enough

The jar of flour will not be used up and the jug of oil will not run dry. (1 Kings 17:14)

- Is there something you feel you need, or need more of, right now?
- When Jesus was teaching His disciples how to pray in Matthew 6, one thing He said was "Give us today our daily bread." Meaning, ask God for what you need today. Take a moment to do that right now. Then make it a part of your prayer time every day this week—asking God for that specific thing you need.
- On a piece of paper write out in a thick, colorful marker, *God is a God of abundance!* Put this up somewhere you'll see it all week, preferably where you feel your need. If you're low on cash, you could put it in your purse. If you're craving boldness, tape it to your mirror, so you'll see it when you get ready to start each new day. If you need patience at work, prop it up on your desk.
- Want to go one step further? Give away a little of what you feel short on—time, energy, dollars (unless you feel Jesus telling you not to, of course) and see how He takes your little (like the widow's flour and oil) and turns it into more than enough.

16

Break the Cycle

Esther

My friend Beth was the first person in her immediate family to follow Jesus. My sister-in-law was the first person in her family tree to get a college degree. Another friend was the first in her family to move away from her home country. Some of us have cycles in our families or within our own personal history. Traditions are one thing. And some patterns or ways of doing things are good, or even good for other members of our family (like my friend's family who stayed in their homeland). But there are some cycles we would like to shake or even break. Maybe it's a cycle of abandonment. Or abuse. Or materialism. Maybe it's a cycle of addiction or loneliness or stifling our emotions or being involved in toxic relationships. Perhaps there's a systemic cycle of oppression or injustice. I was so close to living out and carrying on a bad cycle perpetuated by my family of origin. In Scripture, Queen Esther was a breath away from being trapped in a cycle of systemic oppression.

Esther was an orphan living in Persia. The Jewish people—*her* people—had been held as captives in exile for a century.

> [Esther] was taken to King Xerxes [pronounced Zerk-sees] in
> the royal residence in the tenth month, the month of Tebeth,

in the seventh year of his reign. Now the king was attracted to
Esther more than to any of the other women, and she won his
favor and approval more than any of the other virgins. So he
set a royal crown on her head and made her queen instead of
Vashti. (Esther 2:16–17)

Our orphaned, exiled girl a queen? Awesome, right?

Not exactly. In an appalling roundup of, as King Xerxes called them,
"beautiful virgins," Esther was carted off to become a member of the
king's harem. Abusing his power, the king took turns in his bedroom
with the young women he'd gathered. Even in the palace as a queen,
Esther was basically a sex slave. Sure, it was to the most powerful man
in the nation and in a fancy home, but . . . no thanks. Esther, like the
Jewish nation, was still stuck in a cycle of oppression.

Meanwhile a corrupt court official named Haman was power hungry and bitter toward Esther's cousin, Mordecai, who refused to bow
down to Haman. Haman was so peeved, he twisted the truth to convince King Xerxes that not only Mordecai but all Jews were disobedient to the king and should be killed. The king trusted his right-hand
man Haman and agreed to this genocide of the Jews.

Mordecai sent his cousin Esther the following message, begging her
to convince the king to reverse his decree:

> Who knows if perhaps you were made queen for just such a
> time as this? (Esther 4:14 NLT)

All of Esther's people were going to be executed. But nobody knew
she was Jewish. This once-upon-a-time orphan girl could continue to
hide her identity and stay safely in the harem with pillows, perfume,
and pomegranates. *Or* Esther could step up and use her royal position
for "such a time as this," to break the cycle of oppression for her people
and save their very lives.

Breaking a cycle isn't a snap-your-fingers kind of thing. It is a process of
prayer, community, and bold action. If we turn to Jesus and trust in Him,
our mighty God will show us a way out. But we'll have to be intentional.

You can break the cycle in your family, your history, your origins too. As John Mark Comer says in his book *God Has a Name*, "We can get off the hamster wheel. Reclaim our humanity. We don't have to stay stuck. If you're living under the shadow of generational sin, you live in terror that you'll grow up to be like your father or mother. Listen, what was true of your parents *doesn't have to be true of you*. You can change the trajectory of your family line. Here. Now. With Jesus."[1]

Breaking a cycle isn't a snap-your-fingers kind of thing. It is a process of prayer, community, and bold action.

I broke the cycle of my family's history of divorce. My parents are divorced. My dad has been divorced three times. Both sets of my grandparents are divorced. Also, both of my father's siblings and one of my mom's siblings are divorced. Marriage has tragically not gone well in my family.

Psychology Today states that if a woman's parents are divorced, her odds of divorce increase by a whopping 69 percent.[2] That's 69 percent more than the 50 percent of all marriages that already end in divorce. I'm not great at math, but those odds were not in my favor.

I see how it can happen. I grew up watching my mom settle for someone who was smart and charming but who didn't value and cherish her. I heard similar stories of my grandmothers settling for men who treated them poorly. I felt unlovable and believed I had to settle for someone who was less than ideal, because beggars can't be choosers. And settling seemed to be the norm. A guy I was dating said he wanted to marry me. Dating him numbed some of my pain and insecurity and gave me a fleeting adrenaline rush that someone wanted to be with *me*, of all people. He bought me flowers and took me out to fancy dinners. He was successful and could provide for me. But when I was with him, I felt hindered, lonely, and stuck. In hindsight I can see that those are giant alarms indicating you shouldn't stay in a relationship. If I'd married that guy, there would have been an extremely high chance of it ending in divorce. But at the time, I worried he might be the only person who would ever love me.

So how did Esther break her cycle? How did I? How can you?

The first step is to turn to God.

After Mordecai's powerful declaration that perhaps Esther was made exactly for this, she sent a message back to Mordecai, saying, "Go, gather together all the Jews who are in Susa, and fast for me. Do not eat or drink for three days, night or day. I and my attendants will fast as you do. When this is done, I will go to the king, even though it is against the law. And if I perish, I perish" (Esther 4:16).

I love that the Bible documents Esther fasting before she did anything. Fasting is a way to turn our hearts and prayers to God. The Jewish nation practiced it regularly. *Okay*, she thought. *I can spend a few days in prayer. That's something I can do.* Spending time with the Lord strengthened Esther so she was ready to take the next step.

I wish I could say I was in the best place spiritually and prayed and fasted about my relationship situation. Thankfully, even when we are not, God is faithful. Even though I wasn't seeking God's opinion, God made it clear to me that He had more for me. God whispered to my heart, "You don't have to settle. You should never settle." This revelation was so strong in my soul. But the choice was still up to me. I *could* stay in my destructive cycle. Or I could step into God's invitation of abundance. If I wanted to break the cycle, I needed to listen to God.

The second step in breaking harmful cycles is seeking community.

Esther didn't try to take this on by herself. She asked *all* the Jews in Susa to fast with her. Esther depended on her cousin Mordecai to send this message. She listened to Mordecai's encouragement and clung to it when things got hard. Breaking a cycle is hard work, and we're not called to do it on our own.

While I was wrestling with the toxic relationship I was in, a friend who was wise, a good listener, and someone who made me laugh came to visit me. He loved Jesus and accepted me for who I was. Through our conversations I realized more and more I shouldn't stay with the guy I was dating. Even with God's nudge, at that time in my life I needed someone to ask me good questions and help me process. I believe God sent that friend to me at that exact time. Being with my friend gave me the strength and encouragement to not settle.

The third step in breaking cycles is taking action.

This can sometimes be the hardest part. But if we've spent time with God, seeking His help and guidance, and have enlisted the help of others, we'll be prepared and brave enough to do whatever we need to do.

All right, Esther told herself, *you can do this. Take a shower and put on something that makes you feel good about yourself, plus those robes the king gave you. God is with you. All those people are praying. You can do this.* I picture Esther shaking as she entered the king's hall. Heart racing. Mouth dry. It was illegal to approach the king (even as queen), and she could be killed for such audacious action. *Next, okay, walk into the king's court. One step at a time.*

> On the third day Esther put on her royal robes and stood in the inner court of the palace, in front of the king's hall. The king was sitting on his royal throne in the hall, facing the entrance. When he saw Queen Esther standing in the court, he was pleased with her and held out to her the gold scepter that was in his hand. So Esther approached and touched the tip of the scepter.
>
> Then the king asked, "What is it, Queen Esther? What is your request? Even up to half the kingdom, it will be given you." (Esther 5:1–3)

Things went well. The king wasn't angry; he was happy to see her. I believe her time in prayer and fasting softened Xerxes's heart. Esther invited him to dinner. At dinner she was nervous again, couldn't get the words out, or maybe she sensed it wasn't quite time yet, so Esther invited Xerxes back to dinner again. On the second night, Esther got her nerve up and made the ask:

> If I have found favor with you, Your Majesty, and if it pleases you, grant me my life—this is my petition. And spare my

people—this is my request. For I and my people have been
sold to be destroyed, killed and annihilated. (Esther 7:3–4)

King Xerxes granted Esther her request. He had Esther and Mordecai send out a new order that would grant the Jewish people protection. She'd done it! The orphan girl from an oppressed nation freed
her people from a cycle of slavery and death. The Bible could have fast-
forwarded to when Esther actually asked the king and he said yes, but
isn't it reassuring that Scripture shows us the steps Esther had to take,
how it wasn't easy-peasy? But by turning to God, seeking help from
community, and taking action, Esther saved the Jewish people from
the trajectory of persecution they were currently facing.

I took the first step and broke up with that guy. That didn't guar-
antee a healthy marriage, or marriage at all, but it was an initial intentional action toward breaking the cycle.

And by the grace of God, I married a man who sees me and loves
me like Jesus sees and loves me. Brett and I have been blissfully married for twenty-nine years. We have been blessed. Not because our
relationship is perfect. But because Jesus is. And only because Jesus is
the rock we've built our relationship on, our marriage remains solid,
even in the storms of life. We turn to God first. Brett and I rely on each
other, not trying to figure out our marriage, feelings, challenges, and
triumphs on our own. And we take action to maintain a healthy marriage. We pray together. Have the hard conversations. Listen to each
other. Serve one another. We schedule intentional and regular dates as
well as time away together. When we do selfish and prideful things (as
all humans do), we confess our garbage to each other. And forgive one
another. Give each other grace.

With the help and empowerment of Jesus, I've broken the cycle.

Please hear me: I'm not judging you if you're divorced. Some of
my favorite people have tragically had their marriages end in divorce. I've seen their pain and struggles, and it breaks my heart. For
a few incredible, faithful women I know, ending their marriages to
toxic, dangerous men was necessary to step into Christ's freedom and
break the destructive cycles in *their* lives. My point is that divorce is

a cycle in *my* family I've been able to break with the help and power of Jesus.

You can halt a current trajectory that you know isn't good for you and change directions. You can. Not by yourself. Just like Esther and me, you don't have to do it alone. In fact, you can't. You need Jesus. And you can ask the people around you for help too.

We mess up. We're not perfect. We live in a fallen world. But we don't have to be clean enough, good enough, smart enough, pretty enough, or strong enough to make the change. Jesus says you are enough, simply because He loves you. To prove it, He died on the cross for you and took all your mistakes and imperfections and washed them clean and pure. Jesus ultimately broke the cycle for all of us. He will empower you to live a full life. Jesus doesn't want you to settle for anything less.

So that cycle you're stuck in? The dead-end job or poor financial management or unhealthy habit or dishonesty? That place you feel trapped in, predestined for, where it feels so hard to change or step out or speak up? You don't have to stay there. You can break those chains. Our mighty God wants more for you. Better. You don't have to accept abuse or overspending or overeating or codependency or neglect. You can crawl to Jesus even in pain and suffering and ask Him for help, beg Him for change, follow where He leads, choose Him again and again over what's familiar or comfortable or expected. You can do it with Jesus, whose power is made perfect in your weakness. His grace is enough (2 Corinthians 12:9). He will make you brave.

Esther could have been executed. I could have married someone toxic and crashed and burned in painful divorce. But God wants us all to be free. It is for freedom that Christ has set us free (Galatians 5:1).

Jesus offers you this freedom.

Will it be a piece of cake?

I doubt it.

Ask Jesus for help. He'll hold your hand every step of the way. He wants goodness and freedom for you. Ask friends for prayer or rides or a meal or a hug or the name of a good counselor or help writing a grant, finding an apartment, or spreading the word about your new business.

Perhaps *you* were made for a time such as this—to break the cycle and step out of slavery—whatever it is that's been bogging you or your family down. Perhaps you were made to be the queen who changes not only your trajectory but the future of an entire group or nation or neighborhood or church. Trust in Jesus, and let Him lead and empower you to freedom.

Break the Cycle

It is for freedom that Christ has set us free. (Galatians 5:1)

- Does your family, like Esther's or mine, have a track record of something you'd like to be free from? Do you have a cycle you'd like to break?

  Talk to Jesus about it. Ask Him to take it from you, to help you break the cycle.

  Envision that thing as a chain with a padlock. Now picture Jesus with the key to unlock the chain. Picture it falling to the ground. Do you hear it clanging on the floor? You've broken the cycle. You're free.

  How do you walk into your new life? Spend some time in prayer asking Jesus to give you any ideas on what that first step might be.

- What can you do today to start breaking those chains? Confide in someone you trust about your problem? Google when and where a local support group meets, and put it on your calendar? Make an appointment with a doctor or counselor?

  Do the thing. Take the step.

17

Keep Them Safe

Jehosheba

Most of us are familiar with the story of Anne Frank, the Jewish girl who went into hiding with her family during the Nazi occupation of Amsterdam. But are you familiar with the woman who protected Anne Frank, Miep Gies?

Miep worked for Otto Frank, Anne's dad. One day Otto approached Miep and told her he planned to take his family into hiding and asked if she would help. Miep and her husband not only immediately agreed but also brought food, books, supplies, and mail to the Franks and the other four people (eight in total) who were hiding in a secret annex within Otto Frank's offices. Miep bravely risked her own life several times a day for two dangerous years. Miep and her husband, Jan, weren't just caring for the Franks and their friends; they were also hiding another Jewish man in their own home.

When asked about how she responded when Otto Frank asked for her help, Miep answered, "It was a matter of course for me, I was able to help these people. We did our human duty: helping people in need."[1]

Miep could have been arrested, sent to a concentration camp, or killed on the spot for helping these Jewish friends hide from the

Nazis. But for her, a Christian, it was simply what people were supposed to do.

Almost a hundred years earlier, in the United States, Harriet Tubman sheltered enslaved people on their way to safety via the Underground Railroad. Harriet, born an enslaved woman in Maryland, escaped to Philadelphia and found herself free. Looking back on her arrival to the North she proclaimed, "I felt like I was in heaven!"[2]

Harriet could have reveled in her safety and freedom and never looked back. Instead, she made nineteen trips, escorting over three hundred enslaved people to their own freedom. She bravely risked her life on every one of those nineteen trips. Anyone caught assisting the enslaved could be arrested, killed, or returned to the South, where they would no longer be free but once again be enslaved themselves.[3] Despite the risks, Harriet, a passionate believer in God, knew people were never intended to be property and fought to help the marginalized find the freedom they were entitled to at any cost.

Even further back in time, in the Middle East, a woman named Jehosheba hid a little boy who was in grave danger and kept him safe.

> But Jehosheba, the daughter of King Jehoram and sister of Ahaziah, took Joash son of Ahaziah and stole him away from among the royal princes, who were about to be murdered. She put him and his nurse in a bedroom to hide him from Athaliah; so he was not killed. (2 Kings 11:2)

Why did Jehosheba need to save baby Joash? Because his cruel, power-hungry grandmother, Queen Athaliah, had all her grandsons murdered so none of them would take the throne from her. That's about as evil as evil gets. Fortunately, the wicked queen wasn't able to kill *all* her grandsons. She didn't realize one had been rescued, hidden, and protected by her stepdaughter Jehosheba.

Can you imagine how terrifying it was for Jehosheba to go behind this murderous woman's back? But Jehosheba saw someone in need who couldn't protect themselves. She also knew God's words—"Do not stand idly by when your neighbor's life is threatened. I am the

Lord" (Leviticus 19:16 NLT)—so she bravely kept that little boy safe. When Joash was seven years old, Jehosheba's dad arranged a coup, knocked Queen Athaliah out of power, and crowned little Joash king of Israel.

All three of these women—Miep, Harriet, and Jehosheba—amaze and inspire me. They protected the marginalized at the risk of their own lives, but what do they have to do with you and me?

Everything.

Jesus explained,

> Then the King [Himself, Jesus] will say to those on his right, "Come, you who are blessed by my Father; take your inheritance, the kingdom prepared for you since the creation of the world. For I was hungry and you gave me something to eat, I was thirsty and you gave me something to drink, I was a stranger and you invited me in, I needed clothes and you clothed me, I was sick and you looked after me, I was in prison and you came to visit me. . . .
>
> "Truly I tell you, whatever you did for one of the least of these brothers and sisters of mine, you did for me." (Matthew 25:34–36, 40)

Jesus wants us to feed the hungry, give drinks to the thirsty, shelter strangers, clothe those who need clothes, take care of the sick, and visit the incarcerated. In a nutshell, He asks us to take care of other people, especially the marginalized.

Why? Because they are His kids. He loves them. And just like Jesus wants goodness and health and safety for you and me, He wants those same things for people who can't do it for themselves. He asks us to get in on His good work. Just like Miep, Harriet, and Jehosheba did.

Caring for the marginalized could mean something as simple as having a stash of granola bars and bottles of water in your car and making it your practice that when you see a person living on the streets, you hand them one of each. You'll have to plan ahead and interrupt your normal routines. But you are feeding the hungry and giving drinks to the thirsty. Jesus is smiling. He says you fed Him and gave him a drink too. Well done.

Jesus asks us to take care of other people, especially the marginalized.

It could mean you invite a friend in an abusive situation or in between homes to spend a few nights or weeks at your house to keep them safe until they can find their own place. Sure, you'll have less privacy and less space. But you sheltered a person. Bravo. Jesus is so happy.

Maybe God is calling you to help kids in need. You could get certified by the foster system to be an approved babysitter for foster parents. Or you might sponsor a child in another country through an organization like World Vision International or volunteer locally with Big Brothers Big Sisters or read stories and lead crafts at an after-school program. When you do it's as if you're caring for Jesus Himself. All are incredible ways to love God's children.

You could volunteer for a prison ministry. Maybe baking cookies for inmates or visiting them. According to Jesus, this is also a visit to Him. Jesus loves it when you bring hope to a dark place.

This isn't a guilt trip. We aren't supposed to do *all* these things all the time. If your plate is piled with commitments, you might already be helping those in need. (Often this is people in our own homes or families.) Everyone's situation is different. Some of us have more time but less money. Great. Volunteer. Some of us have zero time but an unexpected bonus check. Wonderful. Donate to a cause you're passionate about. If you're a phenomenal cook, make an extra casserole. Are you an organizer extraordinaire? Plan the fundraiser for an awesome charity, pick the menu, order the decorations, send the invites.

When a sign-up list of jobs was sent out to all the parents for a fundraiser at our kids' school, I clicked the link and browsed my options. Wait, what? Nobody wanted to send the emails? Did I read that right? To me, the writer, writing emails was something I could do in my sleep. Well, almost. I signed up for that position before someone decided that didn't count as an actual job. A week later, another mom who had volunteered to work the ticket booth at the event for hours on end told me, "I'm so grateful you took the email slot!"

Let's just say *I* was so grateful *she* filled her slot. What I'm getting at is: Don't feel bad about what you have to offer. If we all help in the ways we can, with the things we're passionate about, I promise the world will be a better place.

This also isn't an assignment you need to check off your list. *Helped deliver food baskets for Thanksgiving.* Check. Listen, helping a food pantry is a wonderful and gratifying thing to do (it's guaranteed to change your perspective, increase your gratitude, and even boost your mental health). But we don't have to earn our way into God's kingdom. He's already given it to us. For free.

I love *The Message's* version of why Jesus asks us to help others: "Whenever you did one of these things to someone overlooked or ignored, that was me—you did it to me" (Matthew 25:40).

So in the spirit of so many incredible women who have gone before us like Miep, Harriet, and Jehosheba, let's be the ones to volunteer, donate, share what we have, or shelter someone who needs to be kept safe. It might be risky. We might have to give up some time, energy, comfort, flexibility, or money. But we can do what we can for God's people in need. Serving others boosts our sense of purpose and lowers our stress. But most importantly we can do it for Jesus. Because He loves us. And He'd do anything for us. He empowers us to be able to bravely give from what He's given us. Let's help those in need for the glory of God.

Keep Them Safe

Whenever you did one of these things to someone overlooked
or ignored, that was me—you did it to me. (Matthew 25:40
MSG)

- Where do you see a need around you? Anything from an elderly next-door neighbor who would benefit from you mowing their lawn, to going on a mission trip to build houses in a destitute area, or like Jehosheba maybe you know a child who needs protection. Write at least three things down.
- What are some of your strengths or resources—time, money, expertise, an empty room?
- Pray about how and where you can help, then commit to helping someone this week. Write that thing down to hold yourself accountable. Afterward, use the space below to journal about the experience.

18

Answer Their Questions

Huldah

My oldest daughter sends me silly videos of women in their twenties calling their moms and asking about, well, everything. "Mom, how much is too much to pay for a bath mat?" "Mom, I'm a little stuffy; do you think I have COVID-19? Or strep throat?" "Mom, can you make a dermatologist appointment for me?" "Mom, how do I know when the chicken is done?" "Mom, what is my social security number?" "Mom, should I take Tylenol or Advil?"

These videos crack me up because this is exactly what my girl in her twenties does. She calls me with these kinds of questions—some of these exact questions—and I love it. I love it because it makes me feel like my daughter trusts me, like she can come to me. But mainly I love it because I want her to live the fullest life—one where she eats fully cooked chicken and manages her money and relationships well and takes the right pain medication.

I ask *my* mom for tips on how to keep plants alive and how to roast a turkey. I ask my hair stylist how much hair she thinks I should have trimmed off. I ask my literary agent for advice on book contracts. I ask my daughters if I can pull off wearing a certain dress—or not.

Who do you go to for advice? Why?

Who asks you questions? What about?

In the Old Testament we find a woman people sought out for answers to their questions. Her name was Huldah.

King Josiah commissioned a grand project to restore the temple. Most of us have an idea how much a kitchen remodel might cost, but can you imagine a temple remodel? Needless to say, Josiah sent the high priest to count the money to fund construction. In the process, the high priest found the Book of the Law (this could have been the first five books of the Bible or only Deuteronomy). When King Josiah had the Book of the Law read to him, he was devastated. His people hadn't been following God's laws at all, and it broke his heart. So King Josiah directed his men, "Go, inquire of the LORD for me and for those who are left in Israel and in Judah concerning the words of the book that has been found" (2 Chronicles 34:21 RSV).[1]

You know who the guys went and asked?

Huldah.

> Hilkiah and those the king had sent with him went to speak to the prophet Huldah, who was the wife of Shallum son of Tokhath, the son of Hasrah, keeper of the wardrobe. She lived in Jerusalem, in the New Quarter.
>
> She said to them, "This is what the LORD, the God of Israel, says . . ." (2 Chronicles 34:22–23)

Huldah went on for five more verses giving very specific instructions and warnings from the Lord for King Josiah and his people. Josiah hung on Huldah's every word and took immediate action. He gathered the people "from the least to the greatest" and read the entire Book of the Covenant out loud to them (2 Chronicles 34:30). Then Josiah pledged to follow God and all His commands and required His people to do the same. Huldah's immediate, specific, and God-inspired answer made a tremendous difference to an entire kingdom.

Huldah was a prophet, and everyone knew she had answers about God and His Word, that she heard God's voice. Huldah was their go-to girl when they had a question about God.

How about you?

If a friend had a question about the Bible or Jesus or church or prayer, would you be the person they came to with their questions?

Why or why not?

I hope I am like Huldah. I hope that everyone knows they can ask me about Jesus or the Bible and I'll try my best to answer correctly. I hope they know if I don't have the answer, I'll suggest resources that might help them, or dig into their question and get back to them. I hope everyone who has contact with me knows they could ask why hanging out with Jesus matters or ask me for prayer. Because I *love* praying for people. And I'm fairly vocal that Jesus makes *all* the difference. Brett even bought me a sweatshirt that reads, "Warning: I may start talking about Jesus at any minute." Gosh, I love that sweatshirt—and that man.

There was a time in my life when I doubt anyone would have asked me those questions. College-aged Laura put her faith, along with her Bible, under her pillow and therefore missed out on so much freedom and abundance. I also missed all kinds of opportunities to tell people about the goodness of God. God is such a good Father that He has used and redeemed that time in my life to teach and grow me. He makes everything, even our dumb mistakes, work out for our good and His glory.

But even after I was back to reading my Bible and talking to Jesus on the regular, it was a while before anyone would have come to me with questions. I didn't openly chat about my faith. What was I afraid of? People thinking I was weird? Not cool? That they would stop being my friend or inviting me to things? Truth is, anyone who would have dropped me for following Jesus probably wasn't that good a friend to start with, and the things they wouldn't include me in were probably not the best use of my time anyway. I love how Paul addressed others' opinions when we share about Jesus:

If it seems we are crazy, it is to bring glory to God. And if
we are in our right minds, it is for your benefit. Either way,
Christ's love controls us. (2 Corinthians 5:13–14 NLT)

Jesus changed my life. He took me from a place of feeling like I
needed to please all the people all the time and that I would never be
good enough to do so, to a place where I feel loved and valued by Him.
His grace astonishes me. His joy is my strength. His peace surrounds
me. He puts a shield of protection around me. He empowers me. I
don't care if people think I'm crazy. I want everyone I encounter to
know about this life-changing love and grace. I want God's love to
control me, not the opinions of others. A few verses down in Paul's
same letter he stated:

We are therefore Christ's ambassadors, as though God were
making his appeal through us. (2 Corinthians 5:20)

Christ's ambassador.
I love the ring of that.
That's what Huldah was. Are you?

> I want everyone I encounter to know
> about this life-changing love and grace.
> I want God's love to control me, not the
> opinions of others.

Do your friends know you're a Christian, that you read the Bible,
that you believe your sins are forgiven? Do the people you encounter
have a sense that you're living an amazing life that is so much more
than what the world offers? Or even if you're experiencing some really
hard things, do you radiate hope and strength in the midst of them?
Do you claim your faith publicly?

If not, why not? Because if others don't know those things about you, they most likely won't ask you questions about those topics. What if you could guide people you know to never-ending love and grace, but the opportunity is missed because they didn't know they could ask you?

You might look at Huldah and think, *Well, yeah, she was a prophet, so of course she could speak up about God.*

True.

But you're an ambassador—an official representative of Jesus. Jesus invites all of us into this work. Not just Huldah. Not just prophets. Jesus's parting words to the disciples are for us too:

> Therefore go and make disciples of all nations, baptizing them in the name of the Father and of the Son and of the Holy Spirit, and teaching them to obey everything I have commanded you. And surely I am with you always, to the very end of the age. (Matthew 28:19–20)

Jesus invites us to teach everyone about Him. He promises to be with us, to empower us while we're doing it. And sure, Huldah was a prophet, but she also did normal things like you and me. She was the wife to the keeper of the temple wardrobe. Many scholars believe Huldah would have been talented with needlework, patching up this, hemming that, perhaps sewing entirely new garments—she had work to tend to. As a wife in 622 BC, Huldah was responsible for her household—the meals, the cleaning, the care of the family and workers who lived under that roof. So just like us, she had to manage the budget, do meal prep, clean up whatever that sticky spot was on the floor, call the roof guy when there was a leak, and navigate the schedules of multiple people coming and going. Huldah had work and people and things and a family she was in charge of, just like you and me. But also, Huldah loved and worshiped God. She knew His Word and shared it when people asked. That can be us too!

What if Huldah had been shy about her faith or knowledge of God? What if no one knew to go to *her* with questions? What if someone asked, and Huldah downplayed her faith or knowledge?

Israel had turned away from God. Their past two kings had cut off relationship with Him altogether, turned to false gods, and expected the people to follow suit. The entire nation had lost God's laws and didn't even know they were missing. Pagan altars had been built inside the temple, which was supposed to be the place people communed with God. Yes, King Josiah was trying to change all that, but for the fifty-seven years leading up to his reign the kingdom was dominated by pagan worship. It wasn't culturally normal or safe to talk about God. Yet Huldah made it clear who she was and who she listened to, even though that would have been frowned upon and potentially dangerous. Still, people knew Huldah was the one with answers about God. Not to mention that the message from God that Huldah shared about the forthcoming doom to Israel was not a popular one to deliver.

But Huldah didn't hesitate. She made it known in her community that she followed, heard, and listened to the one true God. When King Josiah needed answers, his guys knew exactly where to go. And when they got there? Huldah told it to them straight.

Huldah, like you or me when someone asks us about God, might have had a split second where she wondered how she should answer. She could act naive or blow off the severity of the question *or* tell the truth of what she knew about God. Huldah had studied Scripture and frequently spent time talking to God. That time with the mighty Lord strengthened her. When the moment came, Huldah could bravely choose the noble road. And I believe we can take courage from her example and from the God who empowered both her and us to do the same.

These days people do come to me with their questions about faith. I have led countless Bible studies in our community, posted on social media about Jesus, often asked people if I could pray for them, and covered my laptop and water bottle in Jesus-y stickers. I make it pretty clear that I'm a Jesus girl. And so, I get questions like these:

"I'm struggling with a passage in the Old Testament. Any chance we could get coffee and talk about it?"

"How exactly do you pray with your kids?"

"Why did King David have so many wives?"

"How do I know if God wants me to move or not?"

Yeah, some of these questions are simple, and others are doozies.

I don't have all the answers. I'm not God. I don't know everything. But the love of Jesus is too beautiful to keep to myself. And I have loads of resources available. You do too—study Bibles, pastors, You-Version, podcasts, Christian books, the wise woman in your Bible study, the Bible Project, and Blue Letter Bible, to name a few. We can point people to those resources so they can learn how to discover more about Jesus on their own. We can pray with them to help them hear God's direction or to gain understanding of Him.

I want people to come to me and ask questions about Jesus for the same reason I want my daughter to call and ask if she should be worried about her swollen eye or how much bleach to put in a load of whites—so they can live their lives to the fullest. I, like Huldah, want to be available when people have questions about God and point them to the grace and love Jesus has for them.

How about you?

Answer Their Questions

She said to them, "This is what the LORD, the God of Israel, says . . ." (2 Chronicles 34:23)

- Do the people you see on a regular basis know about your relationship with Jesus? Why or why not?
- Do one thing this week that indicates to the world you're a Christian: wear a piece of clothing or jewelry with a cross or Bible verse on it, hang a cross or Bible verse in the bathroom everyone uses when they come to your house or on your desk at work, or share a verse or something about Jesus or your faith on social media.
- Go deeper: Tell somebody something about Jesus this week. If you've never done this before, it can feel a little wild. But those fears are from the Enemy, because you know what really bothers

that snake? People sharing the love of Jesus. You have Huldah's example, me praying for you, and our mighty God right beside you, empowering you as you take this brave step. It could be as simple as saying, "Gosh, that's hard, I'll be praying for you." Or "Wow! That's so exciting. Sounds like an answered prayer. Praise Jesus!" Or "Jesus loves you no matter what you've been through." Or "Do you want to come to church with me on Sunday?"

If every person who reads this book engages in one conversation about the love of Jesus, think about how many lives could be transformed! Let's do this—shine the light of Jesus and offer those around you a life of love and grace.

19

Step into Freedom

Gomer

The only hope these women have is if someone comes in and rescues them," my friends April and Ryan Berg were told the first time they visited a brothel in India with aspirations of helping the women enslaved there.

Not one person has ever said they want to live in a brothel. Studies show that women and girls who have been trafficked in the sex trade have high levels of fear, memory loss, physical abuse, PTSD, depression, anxiety, and traumatic brain injuries. Sexually trafficking a human doesn't just assault and abuse their bodies; it also assaults and abuses their psyche.[1] Not to mention these women and girls are typically being threatened by their trafficker and feel completely reliant on their trafficker for food, shelter, and protection.

These victims see no way out. They believe their captor's lies that they would be homeless and starve out there. That no one would ever want them. They fear not only that any desperate attempt to escape would be impossible but that they would be found by their captor, which would result in extreme abuse and punishment. No wonder these women created in the image of God need someone to rescue them and assist them to step into freedom.

God sees those women and loves those women. And so, He stirred something in the Bergs' hearts and empowered them to take action. Ryan and April created and run the Aruna Project, an organization that rescues enslaved women from brothels and restores and empowers these ladies until they believe what has always been true—that they are daughters of God, loved, beautiful, and valuable, made in His very image. The Aruna Project begins by having a series of conversations with a trafficked woman. They earn her trust and eventually invite her into freedom. Once a woman is out of the brothel, Aruna provides a safe community for her to live in, mental and physical health professionals to help her heal, and a job as an artisan creating athleisure wear, giving the woman an income, increased confidence, and a sense of value.

Ryan explains, "Success for the Aruna Project is long-term freedom." The organization goes beyond freeing an enslaved woman from a brothel and training her with job skills. They help her create a sustainable life.

In the Bible we meet a woman in the sex trade whom God empowered to step into freedom. God saw Gomer and loved her, so He told a prophet named Hosea, "Go and marry a prostitute" (Hosea 1:2 NLT). So Hosea married Gomer. We don't know anything about Gomer's childhood. We don't know how she was treated. We don't know what lies may have been whispered to or even shouted at her. We don't know how she ended up in that unthinkable situation. Who originally sold Gomer? Under what circumstances? How did they trick or coerce or threaten her? Growing up, had Gomer been sexually abused, maybe even by the men in her home?

We don't know. But, as a woman in that time, Gomer would have been dependent on a male family member to support her. Had her father died? Did she not have any brothers? If there were no men to care for her, she may have been abandoned and a prime target for traffickers. In *Redeeming Love*, a retelling of the story of Hosea and Gomer, Hosea's wife was sold into sex slavery as an eight-year-old girl.[2] Was Gomer's true story similar? Scripture doesn't tell us.

And that's all right. Whatever horrific way Gomer landed in prostitution, God saw her and sought to redeem her. God showed her what love looks like through Hosea, who loved her and fought for her freedom. God rescued her. And that rescue from our mighty God gave Gomer the ability to be able to choose a new, free life. God also comes for us, wherever we are, and shows us what true love looks like, rescuing us from our deepest fears, shame, and trauma and loving us as His children.

Right now, as you're reading this sentence, Jesus loves you and wants to rescue you from wherever you're trapped. He wants to spend forever loving you. He wants freedom for you. God says of His people,

> I will make you my wife forever,
>   showing you righteousness and justice,
>   unfailing love and compassion.
> I will be faithful to you and make you mine,
>   and you will finally know me as the LORD.
>   (Hosea 2:19–20 NLT)

By following God's instructions, Hosea freed Gomer from her brothel life and married her. Together Gomer and Hosea had three children. But after treating her with love and creating a home, family, and life together, after Hosea provided and protected her, we find Gomer committing adultery (Hosea 3:1). What drew her away from Hosea, the man who illustrated God's love to her, and toward this "other lover"?

> God comes for us, wherever we are, and shows us what true love looks like, rescuing us from our deepest fears, shame, and trauma and loving us as His children.

We don't know. But like all of us, Gomer had a set of schemas impressed in her mind. As two esteemed psychologists Bricker and Young write, "A schema is an extremely stable, enduring negative pattern that develops during childhood or adolescence and is elaborated throughout an individual's life. We view the world through our schemas. Schemas . . . are very resistant to change."[3]

The schemas in Gomer's mind must have been ones of shame and low self-esteem. Maybe it was these lies in her brain that led her away from the love of God expressed by Hosea and toward this "other lover." Maybe Gomer didn't choose at all but was forced by the other man into this toxic situation. Maybe she didn't believe she was deserving of anything better.

Schemas are hard to shake. They attest to the impact of the trauma we've faced. It's why the Aruna Project invests in the women it rescues for the long haul—they know these women need to reverse their brainwashing and learn a new life. And that takes time.

Gomer's schemas were shaped by the devastating effects of being sexually trafficked. So even though Gomer was loved by Hosea, it was hard for her to accept Hosea's love and as a result, difficult for her to fully accept God's love. I get it. It's taken me years to shake some schemas that were falsely embedded in me as a child—thought patterns that made me feel like I was unworthy of God's love or anyone else's. You likely have some schemas of your own you might be trying to unlearn.

Gratefully, Gomer and the women the Aruna Project has rescued have experienced what true love looks and feels like. You can too. Because love's name is Jesus. And He longs to shower you with unfailing love and compassion.

The man Gomer was with claimed ownership of her, considered her his slave, and charged a price for Hosea to get her back. Once again, Gomer had lost her freedom and was enslaved. When Hosea came to save Gomer, she couldn't go home with him. So Hosea bought her back. He paid the price to free his bride—fifteen pieces of silver and five bushels of barley and a measure of wine (Hosea 3:2).

Why? Because God told Hosea, "Love her as the LORD loves the Israelites" (Hosea 3:1).

We see Hosea doing the action. But it is God who told Hosea to do it. It is out of God's unfailing love and compassion that He sent Hosea to go back to Gomer. To remind her again how loved she was. To show her again how much value she had to Him. That she was worth fighting for and going back for over and over.

God loves you this much too. God wants to be with you, talk with you, guide you, share life with you, keep you safe, make you brave, and lavish you with affection.

Even if you mess up. Even if you fall back to bad habits or get trapped.

Someone had to pay the price if Gomer was to be set free. God asked Hosea to be that someone. There's a price for all freedom. Someone has to pay for that thing we did, the way we treated that person, the time we said something we wish we could take back or didn't say something we know we should have—all of it.

Jesus loves you and me so much that, despite our sins or schemas or sexual pasts, even when we feel helpless to move forward or break free, Jesus wants to be with us. And just like the Bergs acted on God's promptings to give of their time and resources to free women who are incapable of orchestrating or paying for their own escape, just like Hosea through God's promptings was willing to sacrifice silver, wheat, and wine to get Gomer back, Jesus willingly paid the extravagant price of His own life for our redemption and freedom. His is the ultimate and greatest love.

> But now he has reconciled you by Christ's physical body through death to present you holy in his sight, without blemish and free from accusation. (Colossians 1:22)

And now, God sees us as He sees Jesus—pure, white, clean, blameless, perfect, and holy. As His bride. Who He loves faithfully and forever. That's how God sees you!

Amazing, isn't it?

A woman named Priya was sold to a brothel at age thirteen for four hundred dollars. When she got sick, she was thrown into an alley to die. After she was rescued by Aruna, Priya said, "As I look back, I never

imagined life free from that place because I was a slave there. I tried
to run away but never succeeded. I thought I would have to live there
until death. But now . . . this place, these people, this life . . . Aruna is
where I am meant to be. I enjoy my freedom."[4]

We don't get to hear what Gomer did with her freedom. I like to
think that the extravagant love God showered on her made her brave
enough to return home. Even though it would have been humiliating
and so very hard. Did she help Hosea spread the messages God gave
him? Did she lavish her kids with the kind of love God gave her? Did
she, like Ryan and April Berg, start an organization to rescue other
women who were enslaved? I'm guessing it was something that involved taking that extravagant love she'd received and pouring it out
to others.

We too get to choose freedom. Jesus loves you. He is a safe space.
With Him you don't have to fend for yourself. No matter what happened when you were young. No matter what you've seen or heard or
done or been exposed to. No matter what you've been tricked or co-
erced into or robbed of. No matter if you've returned to a life of sin out
of desperation. No matter if you feel absolutely trapped. Jesus paid the
price for your freedom. He came to set the captives free (Luke 4:18).

You can walk away from whatever you're a slave to—bad behaviors,
harmful activities, trauma, shame, bitterness, toxic relationships, fears,
addictions, worries, or negative thoughts—and step into the freedom
of Jesus's loving arms. It will be a journey, but Jesus will be with you.
Jesus wants to take His bride (yes, you and me) home with Him to
restore and redeem, so each day forward will be one filled with love,
grace, and abundance.

When talking about the women Aruna has rescued, Ryan Berg says,
"The transformation is so significant that you would never guess their
backstory." This is what our mighty God's love does.

Seeing Hosea fight for Gomer, love her that deeply, it would be hard
for anyone who knew her to guess her backstory. God's love changed
how others saw Gomer, which empowered her to see herself differently
too. Not as a prostitute, but as God's beloved. The same can be true for
you and me. You are Christ's beloved, which carries weight, emboldens

us. Makes us brave. Changes the way we see ourselves. When we realize that, we too can step into freedom. Jesus will rescue us from our backstories and schemas. We can live fully in the fact that we are loved. We can breathe deeply, free from whatever used to cage us in or hold us down.

Step into Freedom

> I will make you my wife forever,
> showing you righteousness and justice,
> unfailing love and compassion.
>   (Hosea 2:19 NLT)

- What are you a slave to? Social comparisons? Productivity? Unhealthy habits? People pleasing? Status?
- Is there a time when Jesus rescued you? When you were about to do something dangerous or toxic and were interrupted? When you were stuck in a bad situation like Gomer and someone safe showed up or you discovered a way out?

  Take a moment to acknowledge how Jesus helped you in that moment, how He is still looking out for you and has your very best interests in mind.
- Write this out: *Unfailing love and compassion.*

  Thank Jesus for His unfailing love and compassion, and ask Him to help you out of where you're currently stuck or held captive.

20

Say Yes

Mary of Nazareth

My friend Amy (a.k.a. "my Ruth" from chapter 10) is an incredibly successful children's book author. She's written over seventy books, selling a total of over two million copies! Which is insane, and as a fellow author, I promise, not the norm. Amy also cohosts a chart-topping podcast and is a wife and mom. Amy was going about her life, doing all these things, when God told her to go to law school.

Which seemed to come out of left field. Amy already had a successful career, was in her forties, and didn't have time to add law school to her already-demanding schedule. Why should she do this?

Because God told her to.

How did she know it was God and that He really wanted her to go to law school?

He made it extremely obvious.

One email Amy sent me said this: *What? Am? I? Doing? And yet, I know. I Know. I know God spoke those words to me. I know that the very day I researched the Doctor of Jurisprudence (a law degree) and asked my son about it, my boy had literally just discussed that very thing that day at school. I know that the day my son and I were on campus, and he was hungry and there was only one restaurant open on all of campus and that one restaurant made us walk through an LSAT testing center was not just a coincidence. I know.*

And so, Amy said yes to God. She bought an LSAT prep book, studied, registered, and took the law school admittance test. She researched programs and found a great law school near her that offered a part-time program. Amy applied, got in, and received a scholarship. She started juggling the coursework with her other responsibilities. Halfway through her program two things happened:

1. Her husband had a medical emergency that made it challenging for him to work.
2. She got an email saying that two people had sent Judge So-and-So her resume and a recommendation for her to clerk for him. The judge had reviewed Amy's resume and was impressed with her educational and professional accomplishments and was asking for an in-person interview with her.

Clerkships are typically reserved for law school grads and are highly competitive. Amy didn't put her name in a hat and apply. Instead, without even knowing it, she was recommended by two separate people and invited. Guess what? When God asks you to do something, against all odds, He really does make a way. Just as Amy's family was short on finances, God dropped a job with wonderful benefits in Amy's lap. And not just any job, but one with income that helped make law school possible, one that was coveted and would teach her so much about the law, and make the things she discussed in class come to life. And also, almost immediately after taking the job, Amy got a raise. What? Yup, she got to see God do incredibly amazing things as she trusted Him. He's so good like that.

Was it easy for Amy?

Not a single day.

She had to step away from her podcast and have a serious conversation with her literary agent about her now extremely limited writing availability. She commuted downtown from the suburbs on the city bus, reading law textbooks and studying for exams to and from work.

Two days a week she came home to her teenage son and a husband with medical needs. The other three weekdays she went from work to class, returning home much later. Groceries still needed to be purchased. Her carpet still needed to be vacuumed. She still had books she was under contract to write. Her husband had a variety of doctor appointments. Amy deleted her social life and put all her time and energy into law school, her clerkship, and her family, completely dedicating it all to God and constantly giving Him praise for arranging this or taking care of that.

The opening scenes of the New Testament introduce us to another woman who said an obedient yes to a ridiculously hard thing. If you went to Sunday school, you might picture Mary in a pale blue dress holding baby Jesus in a sweet nativity scene. But we first meet Mary in the Bible as a young teenage girl in the city of Nazareth—which was often stereotyped as a no-good kind of town—when Gabriel, one of God's messenger angels, appeared to her. The Bible says Mary was greatly troubled by this visit (Luke 1:29).

When the angel Gabriel had appeared to Zechariah a few months earlier, Zechariah "was startled and was gripped with fear" (Luke 1:12), making Mary's "greatly troubled" feel like an understatement. The original Greek for "greatly troubled" is *diatarasso*, which looks a bit like disaster, and means to "disturb wholly" or "greatly agitate."[1] This is the only time the word *diatarasso* appears in the Bible. Needless to say, Mary was not smiling sweetly. She. Was. Freaking. Out. (Sidenote: There is no mention of the color of her dress.)

Gabriel sensed that Mary was wholly disturbed and greatly agitated. He had this effect on people. The great messenger angel told her, "Do not be afraid, Mary; you have found favor with God" (verse 30).

I imagine Mary taking a deep breath. Maybe even shaking her head and whispering, "It's going to be okay. It's going to be okay."

Gabriel continued, "You will conceive and give birth to a son, and you are to call him Jesus. He will be great and will be called the Son of the Most High. The Lord God will give him the throne of his father David, and he will reign over Jacob's descendants forever; his kingdom will never end" (verses 31–33).

This sounds awesome, especially when you're a Jew and your people have been waiting for centuries for the Messiah, and suddenly not only is He finally coming but you get to be His mom. Still, you're a teenager, engaged but not married, and that sounds like a humongous responsibility you're not prepared to handle. Oh, yeah, and you're a virgin, so the whole getting-pregnant part seems impossible. Mary asked, "How will this be?" (verse 34). Because really, how could it?

But just like God made a way for my friend Amy to attend and pay for law school, God made a way for all this to go down with Mary. The angel answered, "The Holy Spirit will come on you, and the power of the Most High will overshadow you. So the holy one to be born will be called the Son of God" (verse 35).

God will make a way for the impossible, wild things He asks you to do. But in order for Him to do that, you have to say yes.

Mary answered, "May your word to me be fulfilled" (verse 38), which translates to, "All right, let's do this thing."

> ### God will make a way for the impossible, wild things He asks you to do. But you have to say yes.

We know from the Bible's description of Mary that she had "found favor with God." She must have spent time with Him, talking to Him, worshiping Him. And during Mary's time with God, He had been strengthening her, encouraging her, helping her understand how mighty He was and that He was on her side. With that knowledge Mary could say yes even though she was stepping into some extremely unknown territory.

Amy said yes to law school and then to a clerkship. She could do it because God had shown her time and time again that when He invited her into something, He always provided for her. God had done that for Amy in the past with her family and her writing to help her be brave enough to say yes to both of these new adventures.

The good news here? Our mighty God will also give you the courage to say yes.

My oldest daughter said yes when God nudged her to take a job with Teach for America (TFA). When you accept a position with TFA, you are guaranteed a teaching job but not guaranteed a city, age group, or subject. Which, as a senior in college, sounds uncertain as all get-out. But God took Maddie's yes and placed her in the city that was her number one pick to teach special ed literacy, which is her passion and preference.

My friend Kristan said yes when God asked her to start a new church with her husband and some friends. That church is now our home church and serves so many families in our walks with Jesus.

What is God calling you to that sounds wildly outlandish and a bit nerve-racking? It might be countercultural. You might get pushback. You might have had other plans. But if He calls you to it, I promise He'll equip and empower you to do it. You can be brave because He is strong.

Amy is planning to use her law degree to rescue and protect kids in the foster system. God will use her mightily there. Mary gave birth to and raised Jesus, which ultimately led to the saving of the world (including you and me). Talk about having an impact. I can't wait to see how God will use you where He calls you, how He'll use your yes for your good and His glory.

The journey most likely won't be easy. Mary's certainly wasn't. She had to watch her own son be tortured and killed. Amy's wasn't. She had to juggle work and school and family and give up all kinds of things. But God will walk with you and empower you every step of the way into incredible adventures. Into opportunities that will blow your mind in all the best ways. It can start right here and now. All you have to do is say yes.

Say Yes

And Mary said,
    Yes, I see it all now:
        I'm the Lord's maid, ready to serve.

Let it be with me
just as you say.
(Luke 1:38 MSG)

- What is God asking you to say yes to? What barriers are in the way? Things that make it hard?
- Close your eyes and imagine being Mary. Imagine a powerful, wild-looking being named Gabriel coming to you when you were thirteen (picture yourself in your thirteen-year-old clothes with your thirteen-year-old haircut, maybe even braces), telling you you'll be able to do the thing God's calling you to. Now picture yourself saying yes. Nod your head.
- Try praying this prayer: *Dear Jesus, if Mary could say yes, so can I. I trust that Your plans are bigger and better than mine—that if You call me, You will empower me. I pray for courage to get going, endurance to stay the course, and trust in You and Your goodness and faithfulness along the way. Amen.*

21

Jump for Joy

Elizabeth

When my husband said, "I have the opportunity to teach in France for several weeks and bring you and the kids with me," I should have jumped for joy.

I grew up in Ohio, but France has a piece of my heart. When I'm there, I feel strangely at home. As if I were made to stroll cobblestone streets, eat fresh baguettes from one of the boulangeries found on every corner, drink the thick, dark coffee served in white porcelain cups (with a matching bowl of sugar cubes, *bien sûr*) at every café. I love the language, the style, the absolute oldness of everything there, most of which was built prior to the United States even being a country. Taking our four kids to France—living in an apartment, not just visiting but immersing ourselves in one of my favorite places in the universe—sounded like the most beautiful dream I could have conjured up at that stage in our life. So, yes, I should have squealed and danced and sang and jumped for joy. But do you know what I said?

"Don't say it unless you mean it."

Somewhere along the road I learned to tamp down my joy. Maybe it was after watching *The Nutcracker* in the red velvet seats of the exquisite Ohio Theatre with my mom each December, finally getting the opportunity to audition for this beautiful ballet . . . and getting cut almost immediately. Maybe it was applying to the college I'd had my heart set on since the time I visited my uncle, who was getting his PhD among its brick buildings covered with ivy when I was twelve . . . only to get a rejection letter. Maybe it was the relief and hope I felt when my dad returned home . . . that was dashed when he left our family again. It was probably an accumulation of a load of letdowns that led me to create a defense mechanism of not allowing myself to get excited about joyful possibilities, of not even owning or celebrating joy when it came my way—just in case things came crashing down. Sadly, so many of us aren't fully experiencing the joy Jesus has for us. Myself included.

My friend Nicole Zasowski, who is a Christian therapist and author, told me in a recent conversation, "There [are] things going on in the brain that make us not naturally drift toward joy. For one thing, negative input is just stickier in our brains. . . . We also have this thing called the hedonic treadmill, which means our brains rapidly adapt to joy [and return to a baseline level of happiness]. . . . Our brains get used to that joy very quickly. And then we also have this habit of telling our joy how it can be improved upon." Even if we've had a great day, "very quickly, we start telling our joy what would have made it better."[1] Nicole has also shared that if we've known trauma or pain, it can feel safer not to hold joy than to embrace a joy that might break.[2]

Yuck. I want my joy to be stickier than anything negative that comes my way. I don't want to get used to joy or tune it out. And when I have joy, I don't want to tell joy it could do better; I want to embrace it, savor it, hold on to it. You?

Elizabeth in the Bible shows us how it's done. Elizabeth struggled with infertility for years. In any time and culture that could be painful, traumatic, and heartbreaking. But in the Middle East over two thousand years ago, culture considered a woman who was unable to produce heirs practically worthless.

And then it all changed for Elizabeth. The angel Gabriel visited Elizabeth's husband and told Zechariah they were going to have a baby boy who "will be a joy and delight to you, and many will rejoice because of his birth, for he will be great in the sight of the Lord" (Luke 1:14–15).

And because Gabriel's message was from God, of course it came true. Elizabeth, who couldn't get pregnant and also thought she was too old to conceive, got pregnant. Did you notice what Gabriel said? The baby will be a *joy*. Many will re*joice*. What did Elizabeth do with this joy handed to her on a platter? What did she say?

"I'll believe it when the baby is born."

Nope.

"I'm too old for this."

Nope.

"I've been through way too much hurt to even think about it."

Uh-uh.

Instead, "she went off by herself for five months, relishing her pregnancy. 'So, this is how God acts to remedy my unfortunate condition!' she said" (Luke 1:25 MSG).

Elizabeth relished her pregnancy. And she gave God all the glory.

When was the last time you relished anything? *Relish* isn't even a word I use very often, let alone something I do. I pull the chocolate chip cookies out of the oven. I want one. I grab one and eat it as I finish putting the ingredients away. Five minutes later I forget I even ate a cookie. Or I pause to look at a rainbow in the sky, take a quick pic on my phone, and then continue with my day. I kiss my husband so swiftly in passing I almost miss his lips. But what if I relished these things?

What if I let the taste of the warm cookie, the melty chocolate chips, linger on my tongue? What if I poured a cold glass of milk and sat down, thanking God for creating the ingredients for cookies—cocoa beans, sugar cane, and chickens who lay eggs—not scrolling on my phone or trying to send a text or read an email while I ate but simply savoring that cookie?

What if I stared at the rainbow until it dissolved in the sky, allowing myself to be mesmerized by the red, orange, yellow, green, blue, and violet stripes that blend so beautifully it's hard to know where one starts and another ends? What if I meditated on the fact that rainbows are reminders of God's promise that no matter how bad we get, He is still good?

What if I kissed my husband as I pass him like I kissed him when we were dating? Just saying. What if? And what if I thanked God for bringing us together all those years ago, that there is a handsome man—who loves me even in my worst moments—standing in our hallway?

When good things happen, are we relishing them? Are we giving God glory for them?

Nicole went on to tell me that one way to hang on to our joy is by noting how each of our five senses feels in that moment. So with the cookie, there is the delicious taste of it, yes, but also the way it looks and feels and smells, and I'd most likely hear something while I'm eating too—maybe the timer beeping on the oven or the voice of one of my kids. By noticing all five of our senses in a joyful moment—taking a mental snapshot of it—we can savor it more easily. Or as Elizabeth might say, relish it.

Elizabeth's joy didn't stop at her own pregnancy. A few verses later we see her bursting with joy about the pregnancy of her cousin Mary. Mary came to visit Elizabeth and "when Elizabeth heard Mary's greeting, the baby leaped in her womb, and Elizabeth was filled with the Holy Spirit. In a loud voice she exclaimed: 'Blessed are you among women, and blessed is the child you will bear! But why am I so favored, that the mother of my Lord should come to me? As soon as the sound of your greeting reached my ears, the baby in my womb leaped for joy'" (Luke 1:41–44).

The Message phrases Elizabeth's response as "sang out exuberantly."

Not only was Elizabeth bursting with joy but the baby in her stomach was also leaping for joy. Elizabeth was exclaiming or singing out loud how awesome this moment was.

Nicole explained to me that when we state our thankfulness out loud—thanking our child for how patient they were or the barista for making an especially yummy mocha or our friend for helping us move a piece of furniture—it doubles our joy. When we exclaim our thanks, we get a double whammy of joy. Elizabeth was really onto something.

I want to be more like her.

And we can be. We don't have to muster up joy on our own or settle for half joy. Did you see what happened when Mary walked in the door—the source of Elizabeth's second bout of joy? Elizabeth was filled with the Holy Spirit. That's who empowers us to truly feel and experience joy. The Holy Spirit filled Elizabeth then and fills every Jesus follower now. So yes, we can teach our joy to be stickier by intentionally savoring the moments, pausing to notice all the wonderfulness when joy comes our way, and expressing our thanks to double that joy, but we don't have to do it on our own. The Holy Spirit fills us and gives us the ability to tear down our walls of self-protection and doubt and instead relish in the goodness God has put all around us.

If we ask, the Holy Spirit will prompt us to remember those joy-enhancing tips; the Holy Spirit will make us more aware of the moments of joy, nudge us not to rush past them, whisper in our ears, "Hey, remember to give thanks for that." And with the empowerment of the Holy Spirit, you and I can begin relishing the joy that comes our way. And it *will* come our way.

> The Holy Spirit fills us and gives us the ability to relish in the goodness God has put all around us.

Jesus said, "I have told you these things so that you will be filled with my joy. Yes, your joy will overflow!" (John 15:11 NLT).

If you're lacking joy, you can ask for it. God wants you to experience it. Jesus sent the Holy Spirit for lots of reasons, but one of them is to empower us to find and hold on to joy, so it will overflow in us. Paul told the church in Thessalonica to rejoice *always*.

> Rejoice always, pray continually, give thanks in all circumstances; for this is God's will for you in Christ Jesus. (1 Thessalonians 5:16–18)

And James, Jesus's brother, echoed this declaration that we can always find joy, even in the hardest of times:

> Consider it pure joy, my brothers and sisters, whenever you face trials of many kinds. (James 1:2)

How does that even make sense? That we can have joy both when we find out we're pregnant and when we struggle with infertility? Both when we fall in love and when our relationship falls apart? Both when we're healthy and when our body isn't working how we'd hoped?

I think Nehemiah said it best: "The joy of the LORD is your strength" (Nehemiah 8:10). See, we don't have to fake joy. We can find joy in the Lord. In the truths that the God of the universe intentionally created us for purpose, that He loves us endlessly and promises to never leave us, that He actually wants joy for us and sprinkles it into our lives left and right—in the scent of vanilla, the warmth of a hug, the way our favorite song makes our feet tap, the intricate beauty of a spider web, the sound of laughter, the taste of a warm baguette from the boulangerie on the corner or a creamy café au lait. This joy—it strengthens us, empowers us to embrace our life and what God has for us today, even during trials.

Since this is God's will for us, since complete joy is what Jesus offers, I'm asking Jesus to help me find and hold on to joy today. Want to joy-n me? (Sorry, couldn't resist.)

A crazy thing has happened. My husband has been given another opportunity to teach in France—fourteen years after our original adventure, when I was hesitant to feel the joy but ended up spending five blissful weeks living with my family in Lyon. This time it's for one week, and the kids are obviously fourteen years older. Only one of them still lives with us. But I get to go to France for a week.

And I'm giddy.

I want to relish every moment of it, even the planning and packing for it. And I'm saying it right here: "Thank you, Jesus, for creating this opening for us, for my mom who agreed to stay with our youngest while we're gone, and for a husband who wants to seize this opportunity. Yes, it's so Brett can teach a group of international college students, but also because he knows it will bring me joy."

Brett asked me yesterday, "Are you excited?"

I looked him directly in those blue eyes of his, joyful tears in mine, and said, "So excited! I'm so super excited!"

I even kissed him on the lips—a real kiss, like when we were dating.

Jump for Joy

I have told you these things so that you will be filled with my joy. Yes, your joy will overflow! (John 15:11 NLT)

- Savor a lovely moment. Take a picture of it in your mind—not just what you see but also what you smell, taste, hear, and feel in that moment.
- Thank someone out loud (or with a thank-you note) for something lovely they did for you.
- Remember to thank God, like Elizabeth did, for the thing that made you happy. After all, every good and perfect gift comes from Him (James 1:17).

22

Be Patient

Anna

When the Cathedral of Notre Dame experienced a devastating fire in 2019, I wept. When a news show did a special segment on how the restoration was going four years later, I watched intently. The project included wiping the dirt and ash off every square inch of giant sculptures, which date back to the early 1300s, with bathroom-sized cotton swabs.

Imagine cleaning your shower with a Q-tip! I literally can't. How long would that take? And then consider that clean-up job being the size of the beautiful Notre Dame sculptures! What would it take to motivate me to do it patiently, properly, and thoroughly, no cheating or skipping parts? I mean, I often do a quick wipe down of the counter with cleaning spray and a paper towel, not worrying if I miss a tiny spot or two. But all those stone sculptures depicting the life of Christ? With a Q-tip?

The reporter in the news segment said to one of the restorers, "I think you have to have a lot of patience."

She nodded and responded, "Yes. You have to be calm and know it will take time. But it's a pleasure."[1]

How often do we say that? Sure, it will take forever, and we'll need crazy amounts of patience, but it's a *pleasure*.

This girl doesn't say it enough.

We live in a world where almost everything is accessible 24/7. And we want it immediately. I don't have to wait until I see my friend to tell her something; I just message her. I don't have to wait until I can visit my daughter at college to see how she redecorated her dorm room. She can video call me now and give me a virtual tour. I barely have to wait to receive anything I order. Amazon sometimes says it will be here this afternoon.

And because we're so accustomed to getting whatever we want at the snap of our fingers, we bemoan having to wait until next week for a new episode or grumble if we have to wait behind five people for our latte at our local coffee shop. And that's trying to be patient for the easy things, the little things. But if we have to wait for something important? Not pretty. And usually not so patient either. The "I'm praying for my friend's cancer to be healed and, Lord, could You do that now?" kind of waiting. The "Jesus, I'd really like to know if this book is going to land with a publisher and oh why does this process take so long" kind of waiting.

Believe it or not, we can, like the French restorer, find pleasure in being patient in the process of waiting.

Anna, a prophet, knew this. She was widowed around the age of twenty. Translations vary on if she was eighty-four years old when we meet her in the book of Luke, or if she had been widowed for eighty-four years. Either way, she'd been alive for quite some time, and widowed most of it. The gospel writer told us:

> There was also a prophet, Anna, the daughter of Penuel, of the tribe of Asher. She was very old; she had lived with her husband seven years after her marriage, and then was a widow until she was eighty-four. She never left the temple but worshiped night and day, fasting and praying. Coming up to [Mary, Joseph, and baby Jesus] at that very moment, she gave thanks to God and spoke about the child to all who

were looking forward to the redemption of Jerusalem. (Luke 2:36–38)

Anna never left the temple?

Never?

She'd been there for some people's entire lifetimes. How often do we pray for something once and give up if our prayer wasn't answered? Or even ask others to join us in prayer and dedicate our prayers to that topic for a week, month, even a year but get frustrated, lose patience, maybe even get angry if our prayers don't feel answered?

Anna prayed, fasted, and worshiped God 24/7 for at least sixty, possibly over eighty, years. Anna didn't give up. She patiently kept at it. Day after day. Praying for the coming of the Messiah. Year after year. Decade after decade.

And then one day, Anna was doing the usual. Praying. Worshiping. Perhaps she fasted that day. And she saw Mary and Joseph walking around the temple with tiny eight-day-old baby Jesus in their arms. Anna overheard as Simeon—a man she probably recognized because he was at the temple all the time too—walked over to Jesus and immediately started praising God. Next, Anna told everyone she could that this baby was the Messiah. The one the Jewish people had been waiting for for *hundreds* of years to rescue Jerusalem.

Anna was so faithful. She stayed close to God for decades. And then her faithfulness was rewarded more than she could ever imagine! She got to witness the Messiah, the Awaited One that her people had been hoping and praying to see for centuries. How many prophets had foretold of His coming? Jeremiah, Isaiah, Daniel, Nahum, Joel, Amos . . . the list goes on. We know of so many. And yet, Anna was the prophet who got to see all their prophecies fulfilled.

All those prophets who came before her got to see the previews, but Anna, a woman, whose life as a widow may have seemed desperately lacking to her culture, got a front-row seat to the show. She got to see the One who will renew our strength and restore our homes (Isaiah 58:11–12), who will take our ashes and give us crowns of beauty, who will turn our mourning into joy (Isaiah 61:3), who will find His sheep and rescue them (Ezekiel 34:12), who will give us back what was lost (Joel 2:25), and who will save everyone who calls on His name (Joel 2:32).

Yes, Anna had to keep calm and patiently carry on praying, fasting, worshiping, and waiting for the Messiah for a-g-e-s. But it was her absolute pleasure.

It can be ours too.

What are you waiting for? What prayers have you been praying on repeat? What skill have you been honing that you're itching to put to use? Whose call have you been waiting for? How long until you can get your foot out of the boot? Until your baby sleeps through the night? Until you find a new job? Until your big kid comes home?

How can we be patient in the waiting? How can we keep on going, one soft swipe of a cotton swab at a time, as we clean the entire wall of a figurative cathedral? How do we keep praying and worshiping when we're frightened or sad or stuck or just super eager?

King David gave us a template on how to do this in a song he wrote. Not surprisingly it mirrors what Anna did.

> Take delight in the LORD,
>   and he will give you the desires of your heart.
> Commit your way to the LORD;
>   trust in him and he will do this:
> He will make your righteous reward shine like the dawn,
>   your vindication like the noonday sun.
> Be still before the LORD
>   and wait patiently for him.
>
> (Psalm 37:4–7)

We can delight in the Lord, spend time with Him and in His Word. Anna was doing this. She was praying and worshiping, enjoying keeping company with God. Prayer is talking to God, and Anna did it all the time. Worship is acknowledging how good God is. Anna did that every day too. Are we?

The more time we spend with God, the better we hear His loving voice whispering kindness, protection, and guidance over us. The more we feel His peaceful, welcoming presence around and within us. The more we're aware that He's blessing us right now, in the waiting. The more we're assured that He is on the move, even when we don't see or feel it. We can be honest and tell Him, "God, this is hard. Waiting is hard. I want an answer now. I want healing. I want reconciliation. I want to know what's next. I want to move forward. I want to hear back. I long for an end to poverty and slavery and injustice and prejudice and war. Why is it still going on?"

When something feels hard to wait for, we get to choose. We can keep checking our phones or temperature or email. We can pace around the house or stress shop or eat. Or we can turn to our mighty God. We can ask Him questions and share our emotions with Him. We can ask Him for help and guidance and bravery. We can even ask Him for patience. He's got loads.

We can thank God for all the ways He's answered our prayers in the past—people He's put in our lives, programs He's gotten us into, places He's taken us. When we pause to recall how faithful God has been, it's easier to trust that He'll come through again.

While spending time with Jesus, we can ask Him how we can best use our time in the waiting, what we can do this morning, this week, this month while we wait. We can sit quietly with Him, find a peaceful place like a porch, park bench, or pew and just sit, asking Jesus to show us His love or to help us feel His peaceful presence. When we do, we're usually blown away by His goodness.

> When we pause to recall how faithful God has been, it's easier to trust that He'll come through again.

We can be patient in the waiting. I'm not always so great at this, but it is possible. When we are honest with God and keep turning back to Him, thanking Him for who He is and how He's been there, He will empower us to be patient.

We can persistently keep praying for healing, reconciliation, change, wisdom, discernment, and answers, holding fast to the truths that God wants His people to be wise, full of joy, healed, to make good decisions, thrive, and experience love. This is God's will. He's fighting for us.

When we focus on the ever-present goodness of our mighty God right here, right now—in the sweetness of a strawberry, the nuzzle of a puppy, the glow of starlight—we find we're less concerned with the future.

Just like Jesus showed up that day in the temple when Anna was there, we can trust that He will show up in our lives too. We can go about our days bravely, calmly, and patiently because our God is good, and He keeps His promises.

And someday, when we least expect it, when we're moving the laundry from the washer to the dryer or we're on our way to an appointment, we'll get an answer to one of those prayers we've been praying for for ages. The phone will ring, the offer will come, the person who used to make us so angry won't bother us anymore, the what-if scenario we were worried about never actually happened, the baby who couldn't sleep through the night is now riding her bike. Then, like Anna, we will be able to praise our perfect God for how He came through yet again, and we'll be so blessed we'll want to share His goodness with others. And, like Notre Dame's stoneworkers, we'll realize patiently trusting in Him has been a pleasure.

Be Patient

Be still before the LORD,
    and wait patiently for him.
        (Psalm 37:7)

- What are you waiting for?
    Like Anna, talk to God about it. Tell Him what you're waiting for, why, how it makes you feel, and ask for His help. While

you're chatting with Him, ask Jesus to empower you with patience while you wait.

- Flip through old journals or photos on your phone and note the ways God has answered your prayers in the past. Maybe even make a list. Thank Him for His faithfulness.
- Listen to, play, or sing some worship music, reminding yourself how mighty and good God is. Repeat this time of worship every day this week.

23

Be Yourself

Mary and Martha

I've had two daughters for twenty years. They've been sisters ever since my second girl was born. But one summer they officially became "Two Sisters."

When the COVID-19 quarantine sent the oldest home from college in March 2020 and canceled every soccer practice, game, tournament, service trip, internship, and social event either of the girls had planned for months, my daughters found themselves not only once again sharing their childhood bedroom but also sharing their stories, laughter, and adventures. They became each other's social lives and very best friends.

Maddie and Mallory earned money during that season by doing everything from cleaning out our garage to spreading mulch and planting flowers in our yard. I walked out one day to find the girls in matching gray Miami University T-shirts and black Nike shorts. I made a joke about them "twinning" and got the lightning-fast comeback of "It's our uniform. Two Sisters Landscaping."

When my birthday rolled around, Two Sisters Cakebakers sprang into action. They'd been watching *The Great British Baking Show* every night before falling asleep and were itching to try their hand at homemade buttercream. They baked me the most decadent chocolate cake, complete with piped icing and colorful flowers. This was not a one-cake concoction for them. Two Sisters Cakebakers went on to bake three more birthday cakes during shutdown. Each cake was a marvelous masterpiece of butter and sugar.

Two Sisters Book Marketing helped me launch my book that released that summer—writing newsletters, taking and posting pictures, organizing giveaways, and stuffing envelopes. Two Sisters Deck Staining, well, pretty self-explanatory.

The girls were hilarious. It warmed my heart to watch them work and laugh side by side—learning new skills, delegating tasks, getting the job done. But it was also incredibly interesting.

Because they are so different from each other.

My daughters look like sisters—blond hair, blue eyes, strong soccer legs, beautiful smiles. But their personalities are distinct. One introvert, one extrovert. One prefers pop music, the other country. One an adventurous eater, the other a mac-and-cheese kind of girl. One sets the alarm early each morning. The other prefers to sleep in—late. But together? They bring out the best in each other. When one gets too serious, the other throws out a hilarious joke that gets them both laughing so hard they can't breathe. When one doesn't really feel like "working" that day, the other sets a plan and gets them both in motion. When one doesn't have time to water the flowers, the other hauls the hose around the yard. Maddie and Mallory are actually happier, more productive, and more well-rounded together than alone. One of them sees from one angle, the other from a different one, and their combined unique perspectives show them a fuller representation of the overall picture.

The way my girls complement each other reminds me of Mary and Martha, the OG Two Sisters found in the gospel writings of Luke and John. A lot has been written about Lazarus's two sisters, these siblings who were close friends with Jesus. Martha is known for working hard and providing hospitality.

> As Jesus and his disciples were on their way, he came to a village where a woman named Martha opened her home to him. (Luke 10:38)

Martha was a true servant—the epitome of what Jesus asked us to do after He washed His disciples' dirty feet:

> Now that I, your Lord and Teacher, have washed your feet, you also should wash one another's feet. I have set you an example that you should do as I have done for you. (John 13:14–15)

Speaking of feet, Mary is known for sitting at Jesus's feet, so mesmerized by His teachings that she forgot about her chores. But Jesus didn't mind. In fact, when Martha criticized Mary for not helping her dish out dinner, Jesus held Mary up as an example to highlight the importance of worshiping Him, saying, "Mary has chosen what is better, and it will not be taken away from her" (Luke 10:42).

The two sisters' different ideas of how to best spend time with Jesus are also illustrated in John 12:2–4 and 7.

> Here a dinner was given in Jesus' honor. Martha served, while Lazarus was among those reclining at the table with him. Then Mary took about a pint of pure nard, an expensive perfume; she poured it on Jesus' feet and wiped his feet with her hair. And the house was filled with the fragrance of the perfume.
>
> But one of his disciples, Judas Iscariot, who was later to betray him, objected . . .
>
> "Leave her alone," Jesus replied. "It was intended that she should save this perfume for the day of my burial."

Once again Martha is shown with a beautiful servant's heart and Mary is at the feet of Jesus. In their ancient Middle Eastern society, most people thought Martha was doing exactly what she should—serving a meal. And she was. Martha gave of herself so others could recline. But few recognized that Mary was also serving Jesus exactly as she should. So Jesus stood up for Mary, recognizing that both the traditional and the unexpected way of honoring Him were good and pleasing. He empowered both sisters to live fully in how God had created them.

For the record, Mary and Martha weren't perfect. None of us are. For example, Martha griped about Mary not helping in the kitchen. They were sisters, so I'm sure they disagreed sometimes and had differing opinions about what was best. But by speaking to them both with grace and truth, Jesus helped these two sisters bravely live in their true identities—their identities in Him.

When Mary and Martha's brother Lazarus fell deathly ill, "the two sisters sent a message to Jesus telling him, 'Lord, your dear friend is very sick'" (John 11:3 NLT).

Jesus showed up days after Lazarus died. Martha was the first to rush out to Jesus. She came alone.

Mary came out after Martha, and she came with a crowd.

Not surprising. Because the two sisters were different and therefore had different approaches, including with the loss of a loved one.

But interestingly, both sisters uttered the exact same phrase to Jesus when they saw Him: "Lord, if you had been here, my brother would not have died" (John 11:21, 32).

The two sisters both fully believed in Jesus's power to heal. They both believed Jesus was the Messiah. Just because the gals were different didn't mean one had more faith or one was a better person. Both sisters did their thing, lived as they were created by their Creator to live, loved Jesus, trusted in His power, and tried to serve Him the best they knew how.

Which is all Jesus wants from any of us—that we believe in Him, trust Him, and try to serve Him in our own unique ways by being the people He created us to be.

Mary and Martha were different. And this was an incredible thing. Just like Maddie and Mallory are different and also both amazing. Just like you and I probably approach things differently, laugh at different jokes, get excited about different tasks, have a different favorite color, and have a different bedtime.

We believe in Him, trust Him, and try to
serve Him in our own unique ways by
being the people He created us to be.

And even though my girls are different, and these two sisters were
different, and you and I are different, Jesus loves them, and He loves
us. All of us. John 11:5 tells us that "Jesus loved Martha, Mary, and
Lazarus" (NLT). Probably because they were different. Because they
were the way He created them to be in the first place. Because Jesus
knew, before Mary or Martha were born, the traits He would put in
them that would complement, bring out the best, encourage, challenge, and motivate each other—so that they would be well equipped
to serve people in their home *together*, cope with the devastating sick-
ness and death of their brother *together*, make sense of what they saw
when Jesus raised Lazarus from the dead *together*, share their stories
and grow their faith and live their lives *together*.

The apostle Paul explained to the church in Corinth how our different perspectives and talents and passions act together, like all the
ingredients necessary to bake a Two Sisters Cakebakers birthday cake,
to make the kingdom of God a richer, more complete, sweeter entity.

> Just as a body, though one, has many parts, but all its many
> parts form one body, so it is with Christ. . . .
>   . . . If the whole body were an eye, where would the sense
> of hearing be? If the whole body were an ear, where would the
> sense of smell be? But in fact God has placed the parts in the
> body, every one of them, just as he wanted them to be. If they
> were all one part, where would the body be? As it is, there are
> many parts, but one body. (1 Corinthians 12:12, 17–20)

We are all made in God's image. We are all part of the body of
Christ. But we are all unique. And mighty Jesus empowers us to bravely
live out our one-of-a-kind personalities by reminding us that we're ex-

actly who He intended us to be. That all the parts of the body—eyes, ears, toes, and kneecaps—are important; they all matter. It's actually in our differences that we function better together.

I love the differences in my daughters. I love unique aspects about each of them. I love them both so completely that a single hug from either of them melts my heart. A phone call, FaceTime, or shared giggle with one of my girls lights up my day. I don't love either of them more—I love them both as fully as I am capable of loving another human.

Just like Jesus fully and completely loved Mary and Martha.

And just like Jesus—the one who can raise the dead from a dark, musty tomb—loves me and you fully and completely, for exactly who He created us to be. So let's just be ourselves.

Be Yourself

Jesus loved Martha, Mary, and Lazarus. (John 11:5 NLT)

- Do you have a sister (like Mary and Martha did), best friend, roommate, neighbor, or sister-in-law who thinks or acts differently than you do? List some ways you're different and some ways you're the same.
- Pray for this woman, specifically thanking God for all the unique ways she approaches and does things. Ask God to bless her and flood her with love.
- Thank God for all the ways He has created you to be unique and distinct.

24

Quench Your Thirst

Woman at the Well

Henri Nouwen, known as one of the most inspirational theologians and psychologists of the twentieth century, said that the world determines who we are by

1. what we have and
2. what people say about us.

But, if we live in God's kingdom, we can define ourselves by what Jesus tells us.[1]

So what do you have?

A clean house? A noticeable scar? A great haircut? A jaded past? The corner office? The ability to speak four languages? Really cool boots? An ugly breakup? A scrumptious curry recipe? A car that struggles to start on cold mornings? We all have things we're proud of and grateful for and things we would prefer to hide or get rid of altogether.

And what do people say about you?

She's smart. She's a know-it-all. She's funny. She's obnoxious. She's a great listener. She's too quiet. She's a deep thinker. She sees the big picture. She's great at details.

Most likely people say both good and bad things about you. There will always be someone who thinks you're great, someone who doesn't pay attention to you, and somebody who disagrees with you, your actions, and your choices. No matter who you are.

And yet we tend to let these things define us. We think we'll be "better" if we work for that company or live in that school district or if our child is the star athlete or we get a pair of jeans that look like our favorite influencer's. We believe we'll have more worth if they like our manicotti or the way we managed that meeting, or if nobody knows what we looked like in middle school.

Most of us long to have worth. To be seen. To be enough.

Some days we feel like we're making a difference, like we matter, like we have something to add. Maybe we even put on an outfit and think, *Dang, I look cute today.* But often we question it. All of it.

All these measures of our worth have short shelf lives. There will always be more things we could buy, gain, or achieve. There will always be more people whose approval we could try to win. It's an endless quest.

This world bombards us with the things it expects of us, offering false promises that if we do those things, have those things, we will be valuable—a certain relationship status, a manicured lawn or fingernails, a certain score on the golf course or time on the mile or number of push-ups we can do, and a shirt in this year's hot color. We should be cooking delicious meals and treats while also eating mostly fresh vegetables from a farmers' market, watching that show, reading that book, listening to that artist's new album, and obviously using dry shampoo and drinking tart cherry juice all while having beautiful, intimate, uninterrupted quiet times with the Lord every morning.

But we can't. We can't be *all* those things *all* the time. Not to mention that the things the world expects of us are always changing.

But our search for value doesn't have to be endless.

We see this in Jesus's encounter with a woman who, by the world's standards, had none of the things it told her she should have. And what people said about her? Also not that great.

According to the two metrics Nouwen mentioned the world uses, this woman appears to have had little value. We discover through

Jesus's conversation with her that the woman had five husbands and was now living with another man. No matter how this went down, this means the woman had lived in so many different households, had to move, and most likely had to give up possessions along the way. Was she widowed? Divorced? A combination of both? Life expectancies were short, and men could divorce their wives on a whim. Either situation would be painful, disruptive, and traumatic if it happened once, let alone five times.

What man was she currently living with? He could have been a relative who took her in out of pity since a woman without a husband was subject to homelessness. In desperation for food and shelter the woman could have become enslaved to a master or accepted the subpar version of marriage in their culture, cohabitation, which was like marriage without any of the security. We don't know the details of the woman's circumstances, but they feel stark. Since she'd lost five husbands, it's safe to say the woman felt sorrow, loss, insecurity, uncertainty, and displacement. She'd signed up for companionship, love, protection, and provision, for sharing a life with someone, for the status of wife, of being Mrs. Something multiple times, but it never lasted.

And what did people say about her? What would someone say in your town about a woman who had five previous husbands and was living with another man? Even though we don't know her specifics, they were likely tragic and *not* her fault, but that has never stopped people from talking, from guessing, from judging.

The other women in her community came to the well in the mornings and evenings, when the temperature was cooler, to collect water for their households. While they filled their buckets, they chatted, visited, and laughed together. But this woman came in the middle of the day. When the sun was scorching. When no one could say the judgy or snarky things they said or give her those looks that could be louder than words.

Oh, and did I mention she was a Samaritan?

That doesn't mean much to this Ohio girl, but Jewish people avoided Samaritans. Like, walked miles out of their way on dusty roads without sidewalks to avoid passing through a Samaritan village. Jesus and His disciples were all Jewish. The disciples went into town to get food while Jesus rested at the well (John 4:8). *Why would Jesus stop here?* the disciples wondered. *In this village? Where "these people" live?* The disciples were even more stunned to find Jesus talking to a woman when they returned (verse 27). The New Living Translation says the disciples were "shocked."

But Jesus showed this woman that she mattered. That He saw her. That He had goodness for her. He told her, "If you only knew the gift God has for you and who you are speaking to, you would ask me, and I would give you living water" (verse 10 NLT).

Jesus started a conversation with this woman who had lost so much by telling her God had a special gift waiting for *her*. Jesus said, "Everyone who drinks this water [referring to the water from the well] will be thirsty again, but whoever drinks the water I give them will never thirst" (verses 13–14).

Jesus offered the Samaritan woman something that would quench her thirst. Her thirst for love. Her thirst for belonging. Her thirst for protection. Her thirst for stability. Her thirst for acceptance. He offers this to you and me too. All we have to do is believe that Jesus is who He says He is, our Lord and Savior. And we can drink refreshing gulps of His living water.

After the woman mentioned that she knew the Messiah would come and explain everything to the people, Jesus responded, "I am the Messiah!"

> All we have to do is believe that Jesus is who He says He is. And we can drink refreshing gulps of His living water.

He was the One this woman longed for, the One she'd hoped for, the One she'd dreamed of. Jesus still is *all* of that. For *all* of us. We can accept the living water Jesus offers and drink up. Step out of our worldly lives and cultural pressures and expectations and into His glorious kingdom.

Who we are is who God says we are, not who our neighbors, co-workers, or cousins say we are.

So what does God say about us? My favorite quote from Henri Nouwen is that God speaks over us, "I love you, I love you, I love you, simply because I love you."[2]

Not because of what you do or don't have. Not because of what they say or think. Just because God loves you.

I don't know about you, but I have days where I, like the Samaritan woman, go about my business, avoiding others and what they might say or think about me. Days when my feelings are hurt or I'm feeling sorry for myself or I'm plain exhausted. But Jesus is there with us when someone doesn't like us or doesn't approve or doesn't know our story but has a strong opinion anyway. He is there with us when we're desperate and lonely and sad and feel displaced. He is with us when we labor—whether that's the labor of mourning someone or raising children or filling out forms or running spreadsheets or starting over. Jesus comes to us and offers us living water that will quench whatever we're thirsting for.

I like to think that Jesus planned all along to talk to the Samaritan woman on that hot, sunny day. That when the disciples said, "Hey, we should really walk around, because, you know"—*insert sneer*—"Samaritans," Jesus answered, "No. I have something important to take care of here. Let's go into town." And when they arrived in the village, Jesus said to the disciples, "You go along. This meeting is going to be a one-on-one." As the disciples rolled their eyes and went to look for lunch, Jesus thought, *She should be here any minute. I can't wait to tell her how special she is. I'm so excited to show her the love I have for her.*

Jesus is thinking the same thing about you today. No matter what you wish you had more or less of. No matter how others' opinions make you feel. Mighty Jesus will go out of His way for you. He'll defy public opinion and culture. He'll sweat in the sun. All to offer you a special gift that will quench your deepest thirst and empower you to feel His love. Because as Nouwen says, Jesus loves you. He loves you. He loves you. He loves you. Not because of what you have. Not because of what they think. But simply because you are His.

Quench Your Thirst

Jesus answered, "Everyone who drinks this water will be thirsty again, but whoever drinks the water I give them will never thirst." (John 4:13–14)

- What are you thirsty for today? Connection? Love? Acceptance? Acknowledgment? Forgiveness? Security? Rest? Answers? Someone to see you and understand you like the woman at the well?

  Jesus says if we ask Him, He will give us living water (John 4:10). Take a moment to ask Him for that thing you're thirsting for. Write it out in your journal, say it out loud, or close your eyes and ask Him silently.

- After you ask Jesus, allow a few moments to listen. Is He saying anything in response? God might pop an idea into your head, or cause a sense of peace to wash over you, and likely He'll whisper in your ear, "I love you."

25

Reach Out

The Bleeding Woman

I teach a women's Bible study and see God's amazing life-changing grace in the lives of every woman in the room. The woman who in her earlier years once contemplated suicide but is now a wife and mama, giving life to others. The woman who let anxiety keep her silent and at home for years but who now speaks up in study, setting an example on how to live fearlessly with Christ. The woman who grew up atheist but now gobbles up the Bible, hungry for knowledge about the Lord. The woman with a painful past she keeps hinting at who now mentors college women, speaking truth and hope into their lives. I could go on and on.

How did all these women make the switch—from one way of life to another?

In their darkest, hardest times they had a tiny speck of faith, just enough to reach toward Jesus to see what would happen, if it would make a difference. And it did. He changed their lives.

In the Bible we meet a Jewish woman who had her period for twelve years straight. It was uncomfortable, messy, exhausting, depleting, and dangerous to continually lose blood. She spent her savings on medical advice, but no doctor could figure out what to do. In her culture it was considered unclean to bleed, so during your time of the month, you kept to yourself. But if you had your period for twelve years straight? That meant you had to quarantine for over a decade! Anyone who came near this woman or touched her would have also been considered unclean and would need to go through a series of rituals to cleanse themselves before returning to their normal work, relationships, and so on. Needless to say, people steered clear.

This woman heard about a man named Jesus. That He was a healer. She would never get the chance to get close to Him, because she wasn't supposed to go near anyone, let alone this rabbi. But Jesus was coming through her town.

What if?

What if she approached Jesus, got near enough to just reach out and touch the edge of His robe? She decided to go for it. She was already an outcast, lived in isolation, had lost all her money to medical bills . . . What else could possibly be taken from her?

> As Jesus was on his way, the crowds almost crushed him. And a woman was there who had been subject to bleeding for twelve years, but no one could heal her. She came up behind him and touched the edge of his cloak, and immediately her bleeding stopped.
>
> "Who touched me?" Jesus asked.
>
> When they all denied it, Peter said, "Master, the people are crowding and pressing against you."
>
> But Jesus said, "Someone touched me; I know that power has gone out from me." (Luke 8:42–46)

For the woman who everyone shunned, who everyone avoided getting close to, for that woman, Jesus stopped everything. He could have kept walking, thinking, *All right, great. She was healed, and I'm on my way to save someone else, so I can just keep going.*

But He didn't.

Because Jesus didn't only want the woman's bleeding to stop. Sure, He wanted physical healing for her, but Jesus knew this woman, what she'd been through, how alone and desperate she felt. Jesus knew because He created her, just like He created each of us, and He knows all the ailments of our bodies and souls. Jesus wanted more for this woman than physical healing. He wanted to grant her emotional healing too, wanted her to know she mattered, wanted to restore her life. And so, after making sure everyone was paying attention to the person who touched Him, Jesus called this woman "daughter."

> Then the woman, seeing that she could not go unnoticed, came trembling and fell at his feet. In the presence of all the people, she told why she had touched him and how she had been instantly healed. Then he said to her, "Daughter, your faith has healed you. Go in peace." (Luke 8:47–48)

I hear "daughter" and think of my girls—how much I love them, what I would do for them, how their smiles light up my day, how I would drop anything to help them, how much I look forward to spending time with them.

Daughter. That's what Jesus calls you and me. His beloved daughters who He wants to be with, who bring Him joy.

Jesus went on to say, "Your faith has healed you." Notice it didn't take much faith. We don't hear that the woman had been praying fervently for healing or that she had been tracking Jesus down for months. But in that moment, she pushed through a crowd and reached out.

Do you have enough faith to do that today? For just one moment, push through whatever you're struggling with and reach out to Jesus?

You don't need all the faith in the world. Just a tiny little bit. Jesus tells us, "If you have faith as small as a mustard seed, you can say to this mountain, 'Move from here to there,' and it will move. Nothing will be impossible for you" (Matthew 17:20).

Have you seen a mustard seed? It's itty-bitty.

The women in my Bible study have good and bad days. Days when they're on fire for Jesus and days when the things of this world cloud their view, and they lose hope. You might be like that too. Our faith meters seem to flicker. But all we need is a little faith, as tiny as a mustard seed, to reach out to Jesus.

The woman in my study who had been raised atheist had a stirring inside her just strong enough to ask a classmate, "Why do you believe in Jesus?"

The woman battling suicidal thoughts had the slightest hint of hope and called a faithful friend, who steadied her and reminded her she mattered when she was in a dangerously dark place.

> All we need is a little faith, as tiny as a mustard seed, to reach out to Jesus.

The woman whose past looms over her like a shadow tells me some days it's a struggle to pick up her Bible, but she faithfully does it anyway. She finds that tiny speck of faith and reads the words of truth to drown out the lies of the Enemy and silence the shame of her past. She fills herself up with God's promises.

When these women took that tiny mustard seed of faith and planted it, our mighty Jesus made them brave enough to reach out, keep going, try again, take another breath.

The woman in the crowd had just enough faith to give Jesus a try—to take that step forward, to stretch out her arm. And immediately she was healed. She no longer had to worry about spending every coin she had on doctors. She would be able to visit with people she hadn't seen in twelve years! She was no longer an outcast but part of God's family. This woman was now free to be part of society, engage in relationships, and worship in community. The years of isolation that had certainly taken a toll on her mental health were over. Jesus told her it was this faith, this teeny tiny ounce of faith, that made her well. If it was her faith that was the catalyst for Jesus to heal her, think how much her faith grew that day! I imagine she trusted in the Lord and encouraged others to do so for the rest of her life, no matter what came her way. Because she knew firsthand that a seed of faith—it's all you need. It changes everything. Because Jesus loves you, His daughter. And He wants to restore you. He'll take that seed of faith and empower you to thrive.

All Jesus's mighty power and goodness, all His love and acceptance, and all His strength and bravery are ours. We are already His daughters—the heirs of the one true King. When we reach out to Him, we are accepting what's been waiting for us all along. Let that sink in. Accept this amazing grace and live as if it's yours. Because it is. When you reach out, Jesus and all His goodness will always be there for you. You are His beloved daughter, and nothing and no one can change that.

Reach Out

If you have faith as small as a mustard seed, you can say to this mountain, "Move from here to there," and it will move. Nothing will be impossible for you. (Matthew 17:20)

- What are you struggling with today?
  How is your faith regarding this struggle?
- Google an image of a mustard seed. Seriously. Do it. Draw it here in this space.

- I'm guessing if you're reading this, your faith is at least as big as that seed. Reach out to Jesus with your grain of faith like the bleeding woman did. Ask Him to heal you, move your mountain, restore you, notice you, pull you back up. And then listen as He tells you how important you are to Him. How He loves you. And let His amazing grace flood you.

26

Rise Up

Jairus's Daughter

In the song "My Shot" from the musical *Hamilton*, the lyrics instruct us to tell our brothers and sisters to "rise up" and ask when the colonies are going to "rise up," and finally the characters Alexander Hamilton, Marquis de Lafayette, Hercules Mulligan, and John Laurens declare they are all going to "rise up."

I'm a *Hamilton* fan, and this moment in the musical is inspiring. It makes me want to rise up out of whatever is holding me down and do something meaningful.

It's the call to action we hear all over our culture, from mantras of Wash Your Face to Slay the Day to Shake It Off. I mean, sure, we want to do all those things. We want to get up and get going and not let a dang thing keep us down.

But it's not that easy.

Throughout my life I've tried. When my dad left our family when I was young, I tried to rise up and get all A's and follow the rules and keep quiet to show him I was a good girl, that if he came back, he shouldn't leave again, and to show myself that I could handle it, to prove that I was okay.

When my high school boyfriend and I broke up, I tried to rise up again. This time I decided to become a full-on flirt, because I was fine with the breakup. Right? I could rise above it and have fun and go out and get other guys to like me. It was a horrible strategy, but at the time it felt like a way I could attempt to shake off the breakup.

After college I moved to Atlanta, confident I'd get a job in advertising. There was a recession, and jobs were scarce. After a slew of interviews and rejections and a year of working retail and waiting tables to pay my bills, I landed a dream job in marketing. In this position, I tried to rise up again. I meticulously planned professional outfits, arrived at my office early and left late, throwing myself into the work. I could rise above the previous rejections and prove to myself and the world that I had value, that I'd always been capable of a thriving career. Couldn't I?

The problem with trying to rise up on our own or pull ourselves up by our bootstraps or shake it off is it's way easier to say than do. And even if we muster up the strength or courage to rise for a while, it's difficult to sustain. Another argument or expense or insult or rejection can knock us off our feet all over again.

How can the woman whose husband cheated on her simply "shake it off"? How can you wake up the morning after someone you love has died and "slay the day"? How can you just wash the pain of abuse or trauma off your face?

You can't. Not on your own.

I was finally able to rise up when I stopped trying to do it by myself and begged Jesus to help me. And then slowly, little by little, I learned how to stand again, not on my accomplishments or relationships or strength or willpower but on the loving, powerful, steadfast faithfulness of my Savior.

For a girl in the Bible, it was the same. She was totally down for the count. There was no way she could get up on her own—no matter what she or anyone else did. But then Jesus pulled her to her feet.

Her dad, Jairus, approached Jesus in a large crowd and begged Him to heal his dying daughter (Mark 5:22–23). Jesus had compassion and went with Jairus. But remember they were in a giant crowd and had to make their way through. Immediately after Jesus agreed to go with

Jairus, the bleeding woman reached out and touched the hem of His robe. As we talked about in the last chapter, this was an important moment. Jesus wanted to honor, heal, and restore that woman, so He took His time with her. Let her know He loved her. That she had value. Meanwhile . . .

> While Jesus was still speaking [to the bleeding woman], some people came from the house of Jairus, the synagogue leader. "Your daughter is dead," they said. "Why bother the teacher anymore?"
>
> Overhearing what they said, Jesus told him, "Don't be afraid; just believe." (Mark 5:35–36)

With that, Jesus, Peter, James, and John walked with Jairus to his house. What was Jairus thinking as they walked through the streets? Jesus told Jairus to "just believe." I'm sure he wanted to, but could he fully? When they arrived, everyone was weeping over the loss of Jairus's daughter.

> [Jesus] went in and said to them, "Why all this commotion and wailing? The child is not dead but asleep." But they laughed at him. . . .
>
> He took her by the hand and said to her, "*Talitha koum!*" (which means "Little girl, I say to you, get up!"). Immediately the girl stood up and began to walk around (she was twelve years old). At this they were completely astonished. (verses 39–42)

The little girl died.
Jesus told her to get up.
And she did.
The girl couldn't work harder. She couldn't be faster or eat healthier or be more productive or do better or achieve one more thing. She was dead.
We put so much pressure on ourselves to get ourselves up. But Jesus

takes all that pressure off. He says, "My grace is sufficient for you, for my power is made perfect in weakness" (2 Corinthians 12:9). Jesus reminds us we don't have to do this in our own strength. Can you hear Jesus speaking to your heart, "Rise up, little girl. You can be brave. I've got you. I'm the one pulling you up."

No matter how far down you've fallen, how much you're struggling to stand, how heavy the weight is that's keeping you down, Jesus can empower you to rise up and walk around.

If you're anything like me, you want Jesus to do it exactly how He did it for that little girl. You want Him to say, *"Talitha koum,"* and immediately you want to be able to shake off and wash off and rise up.

> No matter how far down you've fallen, how much you're struggling to stand, how heavy the weight is that's keeping you down, Jesus can empower you to rise up.

Sometimes it works like that. You encounter Jesus and throw down whatever you're addicted to and move forward into His light and grace. You're miraculously healed of a physical or mental ailment. The check arrives and gets you out of debt. The person who was tormenting you leaves town. But more often it's a process.

For me, it's taken years of praying, reading God's Word, seeing the Christian counselor God nudged me to see, and sharing hard memories and false narratives with my closest, most trusted friends to be able to rise up. To fully believe how much Jesus loves me, that He'll never leave me, that I don't have to prove myself to Him.

Yet even when we rise, sometimes we still fall.

A trigger. A memory. A setback.

Personally, any of those things could send me spiraling downward. But Jesus has His loving hand on me. He has it on you too. No matter what comes our way. He's there beside our figurative beds when we're unable to stand. He loves, encourages, and empowers us to share with someone we trust one thing about our struggle, send that text for help, attend one more AA or Al-Anon meeting, set boundaries that protect us. Jesus will put the right verse, sermon, conversation with a friend, movie, or book in front of us just when we need it to help us get back on our feet.

Jesus urged me to make the worship song "Good Good Father" my morning alarm sound. I wake up daily to the reminder that God is pleased with me and His love for me just gets deeper and deeper. It's a repeated reminder to rise up and get out of bed and bravely face the day, not as a rejected little girl or someone who has to pretend she's resilient to prove her worth, but as a fully loved child of God. No matter what lies I was told or believed.

Yes, the world will try to keep knocking us down.

But the good news is mighty Jesus continues to call and empower you and me to bravely *"Talitha koum"* daily.

This passage about the little girl Jesus raised from the dead reminds me so much of Psalm 40:1–3:

> I waited patiently for the LORD;
>   he turned to me and heard my cry.
> He lifted me out of the slimy pit,
>   out of the mud and mire;
> he set my feet on a rock
>   and gave me a firm place to stand.
> He put a new song in my mouth,
>   a hymn of praise to our God.

This is what Jesus does. He turns toward us, hears our cries, and lifts us out of pit after slimy pit. Jesus pulls us out of the mud, cleans us up, sets our feet on the firm rock that is Him. And as we rise up, Jesus gives us a new song to sing. Not one of loneliness, betrayal, anxiety, or defeat. But of praise—a song of joy and love. Of something way more powerful than anything holding us down. And as we rise up and walk around in our free and unfettered state, we are a beautiful testimony to others of what Jesus can do, that they have this hope also, a hope to rise above whatever bogs them down. They will be like the people at that little girl's house—astonished.

This is how we were meant to live. Up. Revived. Alive.

I had *talitha koum* tattooed on my right ankle so I can hold on to this truth, see it every day. But even if I didn't, Jesus would continue to tell me, "Little girl, get up! I have so much for you. An abundant life. I have love with no strings attached, with endless grace, joy, and peace. Get up! I'll empower you to stand." He's calling this exact same thing to you.

Ready to rise?

Rise Up

He took her by the hand and said to her, "*Talitha koum!*" (which means "Little girl, I say to you, get up!"). Immediately the girl stood up and began to walk around (she was twelve years old). (Mark 5:41–42)

- What is Jesus calling you to rise up from today?
- What obstacles are in your way?

Spend a moment considering that the little girl was dead. Talk about obstacles! Ask Jesus to remove anything that's keeping you from standing.

Ask Him to empower you to get up!

27

Find Refuge

The Woman They Wanted to Stone

Bundled in coats and hats and with a giant red-and-black plaid fleece blanket draped over our laps, we cheered for our oldest daughter. It was so cold that late October day I was thankful for my youngest tucked in between my husband and me and the heat coming from his tiny body. I sat on the edge of my seat as I cheered for my daughter to play well, prayed she'd stay injury-free, and hoped her team would win—not for me, but so my girl would be flooded with joy. Then a rapid and overwhelming blitzkrieg of emotions hit me.

Not because of anything on the soccer field but because of someone who showed up. It's a free country. And admittance to the games was only six dollars. Almost anyone could attend. This person who had caused me trauma sat next to me and acted like everything was lovely between us. This false front of normalcy triggered my anxious thoughts. And the longer they sat so close to me, the more I was reminded of what they'd done and said, of how their actions affected me, and my anxiety ramped up.

My husband was polite and said hello to the person. Meanwhile my body stiffened and heart raced. My thoughts were lightning fast. *Try to act casual, unaffected. I can't confront them here at my daughter's game . . . not to mention I'm terrible at confrontation in general. I think I might throw up. I don't want them to have access to my girl after the game or my little boy snuggled next to me.* I braced myself for a painful barb or criticism.

I knew I couldn't erase the past or make this person vanish. But I could pray. So I did. Fervently. I asked Jesus to protect me, to come between me and this person, to keep me from harm, to protect my kiddos too.

I trained my eyes forward, keeping this person out of my sight line. But then they asked me something about the team's record or the name of the girl playing center back or another random soccer-related fact. And out of politeness, I turned to respond. I can't recall the question or my answer, because as I twisted my body to deliver my response, I saw Jesus. Like, *literally* saw Jesus sitting in the bleachers between me and this person, in the small space where no one had been before. Jesus dressed like a modern fan for a chilly soccer game, but Jesus—without question, Jesus—not saying a word, but just looking at me with calm, loving eyes, letting me know He was there, that the unexpected and unwelcome person could not hurt me today. They would have to go through Him first.

I know it sounds unbelievable, as I recount the story here. It sounded crazy when we got to our car after the game and through tears, I relayed the whole thing to my husband. Overwhelmed with the fact that Jesus would do that for me, defend me so personally, come to my rescue. Yes, I know Scripture tells us Jesus is a rescuer and a defender, but He was right there on the cold aluminum bleachers offering me refuge when I needed Him.

If you're struggling to get your head around my story, take it from a woman in the Bible. At the moment she was in grave danger, Jesus provided the protection she needed.

> At dawn [Jesus] appeared again in the temple courts, where all the people gathered around him, and he sat down to teach them. The teachers of the law and the Pharisees brought in a woman caught in adultery. They made her stand before the

group and said to Jesus, "Teacher, this woman was caught in
the act of adultery. In the Law Moses commanded us to stone
such women. Now what do you say?" They were using this
question as a trap, in order to have a basis for accusing him.
(John 8:2–6)

You might read this woman's story and think it has nothing to do
with mine. Although hers is way wilder, we actually share some simi-
larities. Let's take a closer look.

The woman was about to be executed by people throwing rocks at
her. Like me, her heart was probably pounding, and her thoughts were
most likely whirling inside her head. *When are they going to start the stoning? How long does it take to die from stoning? Do you die from the pain?
The suffocation of all those rocks? Blows to the head? A thousand painful
pelts? Why didn't the Pharisees drag the man here? According to Mosaic law
he should also be stoned for this. What is this rabbi named Jesus going to say?*

I think Jesus surprised everyone with His actions:

But Jesus bent down and started to write on the ground with
his finger. When they kept on questioning him, he straightened up and said to them, "Let any one of you who is without
sin be the first to throw a stone at her." Again he stooped
down and wrote on the ground. (John 8:6–8)

I'm sure the woman was panicked, wondering, *What is He writing
in the dust? Oh no oh no oh no! He said something about going ahead and
throwing the first stone.*

I picture the woman scrunching her entire body into itself, duck-
ing her head, and putting up her arms to protect her skull. Holding
her breath. There was nothing in her power to do but pray this rabbi
would protect her somehow. And then, instead of a barrage of sharp,
heavy stones . . . nothing. Did she peek out of one eye? Squint to see
what was going on? And see Jesus looking at her not with judgment
or disappointment? Not with a sense of urgency but a calm gaze filled
with love and grace?

At this, those who heard began to go away one at a time, the older ones first, until only Jesus was left, with the woman still standing there. Jesus straightened up and asked her, "Woman, where are they? Has no one condemned you?"

"No one, sir," she said.

"Then neither do I condemn you," Jesus declared. "Go now and leave your life of sin." (John 8:9–11)

Can you imagine her astonishment when, instead of hurling rocks at her, the Pharisees walked away?

This woman knew she'd been caught. Even if it was the man's fault, even if she was being trafficked, even if it was assault (all horrific possibilities), there was no question the couple had been having sex and weren't married. The law said that meant stoning. And yet?

Jesus's very presence provided refuge for the woman that day.

He didn't fight off the angry crowd or wrestle the rocks out of their hands. He simply stated that no one could go after this woman without going through Him, without having a clean slate, which can only be obtained by Jesus's amazing grace.

> Jesus's very presence provided refuge for the woman that day.

The hurt and pain the woman braced herself for never came. All that anxiety and crush of emotions slowly ebbed. Jesus kept the woman they wanted to stone safe when safety seemed completely out of reach. He sheltered me in a similar way at that soccer game.

And He'll do the same for you.

It's who He is. I love how King David said it in this psalm:

Keep me safe, my God
For in you I take refuge.

> . . . I keep my eyes always on the LORD.
> With him at my right hand, I will not be shaken.
>
> (Psalm 16:1, 8)

Where do you feel like you're in the line of battle? Without a shield? Exposed?

Maybe, like me, you'll be in the same place as so-and-so.

Or perhaps, like the woman, you're terrified of getting caught or you fear you're close to getting caught or you've already been caught.

Or maybe it's something else altogether. Maybe you're afraid of what will happen if you can't pay the bill, if the scan comes back positive, if nobody shows up, if they don't love you back. You might feel utterly defenseless.

We live in a broken world. There is pain here. And fear too. But Jesus has overcome pain and fear. He has overcome the world (John 16:33). When we call out to Him, He will shelter us—maybe physically, or maybe emotionally or spiritually. He is with us always. And not because of anything we did. But just because He loves us. I felt helpless at that soccer game. I sat there nauseous, unable to think straight, let alone defend myself.

That woman they wanted to stone? She was probably naked, completely exposed. No one questioned if she was guilty or not. She was literally caught in the act. She couldn't clean up or put on a cute outfit or get some witnesses to stand up for her. She was most likely in fight-or-flight mode. The woman didn't have the courage or words or wherewithal to ask Jesus to forgive her. He did. Later. But first He defended and protected her. He'll do the same for us. When we can't defend ourselves, maybe even when we've put ourselves in a dangerous situation, Jesus shows up in the midst of the peril at hand, and His presence changes things. When we can't protect ourselves, Jesus is our refuge. Even when we make horrible decisions that can hurt us—physically, emotionally, mentally, spiritually. Even when the unthinkable happens, when we might be afraid, we don't have to be shaken. We can be brave because Jesus is right by our side, providing shelter.

Jesus didn't keep that person from showing up at the soccer game, but His mighty presence let me know I would be okay. It flooded me with peace and gave me the strength and courage I needed to sit through the rest of that game. Jesus didn't keep that angry mob from humiliating that woman. But His words and mighty presence protected her and made her brave enough to go and change her life. No matter what state we're in. No matter what we have or haven't done. He is our refuge.

Find Refuge

With him at my right hand, I will not be shaken. (Psalm 16:8)

- Where do you, like the woman they wanted to stone, feel unsafe or vulnerable?
  Call out to Jesus. Ask Him to shelter you. Sit in silence. Picture His face. Picture Him placing a shield of protection around you. You might even want to draw a stick person version of yourself with a giant shield guarding you.
- How does picturing Jesus's presence change your view of the circumstance or the trouble that surrounds you?
- Thank Jesus for the refuge He provides.

28

Go and Tell Them

Mary Magdalene

Joan of Arc is the patron saint of France. This means the home of croissants and the Eiffel Tower considers Joan of Arc its heavenly protector. How did she get such a high status? It all started in 1428 when Joan heard God telling her He had chosen her to lead France in victory against England. Which might make sense if she were a warrior or a soldier. But she was a poor sixteen-year-old girl. And way back then it was against the law for females to be in the French military. Who was going to listen to Joan?

Filled with passion to speak the message God gave her, Joan convinced a reluctant escort to take her to King Charles VII. Against all odds, Joan gained audience to the king, told him things only God would know, and convinced the king of her divine mission. Amazed by Joan's message and hopeful in her certainty that France would overtake their oppressors, King Charles had a special suit of armor designed for Joan. She chopped her hair, dressed like a man, and fought in the Hundred Years' War. Joan helped France take down England, regain their land, and as a result aided King Charles in reclaiming his crown.

A teenage farm girl who obeyed God and spoke the words He asked her to speak saved the day for France and its king. Even though Joan of Arc had zero credentials or experience. Even though it meant approaching the king. Even though it was a rough journey to even get to the king. Even though King Charles would never listen to her. Even though everyone thought she was crazy. Even though it eventually cost Joan of Arc her life.

Have you ever felt God nudging you to say something that was hard?

Like confront someone you love about their bad decision-making? Or ask for help?

Or tell a racist or rude family member, "Don't say that. That's inappropriate. Not in my house."

Or share how God did something in your life to someone who mocks your faith?

Or stand up to a bully?

Was it scary? Did it seem crazy? Did you do it—tell that person—or could you not bring yourself to speak the words?

Maybe God is nudging you today to tell your boss you need to quit your job or call out a friend who's making excuses or speak up for the marginalized or raise an issue at the upcoming meeting. And you know it might be hard. It would be easier not to say the thing or grab the microphone. But you also know God is instructing you to speak, and you might even understand why He wants that message delivered. But really? You?

If you're feeling the nudge today, are you ready to speak? Or do you need some encouragement? Mary Magdalene has been in our shoes. That first Easter Sunday Mary Magdalene was there at the garden tomb. She was the first person to see the risen Lord! And Jesus had an important message He wanted her to share.

> Jesus said, "Do not hold on to me, for I have not yet ascended to the Father. Go instead to my brothers and tell them, 'I am ascending to my Father and your Father, to my God and your God.'"

Mary Magdalene went to the disciples with the news: "I

have seen the Lord!" And she told them that he had said these things to her. (John 20:17–18)

She [Mary Magdalene] went and told those who had been with him and who were mourning and weeping. When they heard that Jesus was alive and that she had seen him, they did not believe it. (Mark 16:10–11)

Mary Magdalene saw the resurrected Jesus, whole and restored! She touched Him. And spoke with Him. Then Jesus gave Mary Magdalene instructions to go and tell the disciples something that would blow their minds. She did as she was told, but the men she'd been traveling and eating meals and listening to Jesus with for a couple of years didn't believe her.

Why not?

Because people doubt.

Because what Mary Magdalene told the disciples was so incredible. It sounded too good to be true and extremely far-fetched. The disciples knew Jesus was dead, buried behind a giant stone. How could He be alive? How could Mary Magdalene be so sure? What had she seen? Had she actually talked to Him? Did she just want it to be true so much that she believed it?

But no matter how many of the disciples doubted her, no matter what their questions were, Mary Magdalene knew. She knew she'd seen Jesus, touched Jesus, talked to Jesus, and she knew Jesus told her to go and tell the others that He was alive.

Mary Magdalene had seen Jesus do miraculous things before. He had cast seven demons out of her and changed her entire life. She witnessed Jesus heal and feed enormous crowds of people. Nothing was impossible with the Jesus she knew and followed. Mary Magdalene heard His teachings firsthand, left her home to travel with Jesus (Mark 15:40–41), and gave from her own resources to help fund His ministry (Luke 8:2–3).

Mary Magdalene was there at Jesus's crucifixion when "the earth shook, rocks split apart, and tombs opened" (Matthew 27:51–52 NLT).

Matthew 27:54 tells us, "The Roman officer and the other soldiers at the crucifixion were terrified by the earthquake and all that had happened. They said, 'This man truly was the Son of God!'" (NLT). If that's what the pagan Romans were thinking, I can't imagine how much Mary Magdalene's already loyal and passionate faith in Jesus was strengthened. She saw Jesus give His life on that cross, and she also felt the ground under her feet shift and shake.

Mary Magdalene was there when Joseph of Arimathea wrapped Jesus's body, placed it in a new tomb, and rolled a rock in front of it. All four gospels mention the women who were there at Jesus's crucifixion and burial. Mary Magdalene knew better than most that

1. Jesus was dead and buried, and
2. Jesus was a man—but also the Son of God.

Early Sunday morning when Mary Magdalene (and the other Mary) visited Jesus's tomb, they experienced yet another earthquake *and* saw an angel. When the guards saw this angel, they were so terrified they fainted, but not either of the Marys. They were afraid, sure, but also "filled with great joy" (Matthew 28:8 NLT).

The male disciples who wouldn't listen to Mary Magdalene missed *all* of this—the crucifixion,[1] the earthquake, the burial, the giant rock preventing anyone from getting in or out of that tomb, the *second* earthquake, and an angel that made trained soldiers faint. But our girl Mary Magdalene saw it all. Did God give her these extra experiences to strengthen her belief? To empower her to boldly go and tell the disciples as Jesus instructed her? Maybe.

Or maybe Mary Magdalene was already so all in that she would bravely do anything Jesus asked her. Maybe that's why Jesus picked her out of all His followers to be the first person to declare the gospel—the good news that He had once and for all conquered sin and death. Either way, Jesus had faith in Mary Magdalene to deliver His message. Back when Jesus first freed her from all those demons, He was growing and strengthening her faith. Now He was asking her to go and tell the disciples that He had risen. Jesus fully believed

Mary Magdalene would and could do it, because He had empowered her to do so.

Jesus will empower you and me to bravely speak what He calls us to speak too. He'll give us the words, the opening, the pause in the conversation, the opportunity. He'll give us an escort or open a door or make sure we have a moment alone with the person we're supposed to tell.

Joan of Arc traveled across the French countryside during a war. Mary Magdalene traveled the streets of Jerusalem—and beyond, as legend has it—spreading the good news during a time when Jesus followers were on most-wanted lists.

Where is God calling you to speak the words He's given you?

Joan of Arc knew it would be near impossible to convince the king that God sent her. Mary Magdalene knew that what she was going to tell the disciples sounded unbelievable. Who is it going to be difficult to convince of the message God has put on your heart?

Jesus will empower you and me to bravely speak what He calls us to speak.

Mary Magdalene didn't want to leave Jesus. She was so thrilled to see Him! I'm guessing it was hard for Joan to leave her family and home. Who or what might you have to leave to deliver your God-given message?

Do you trust Jesus? If He's asking you to say something, do you believe He'll empower you to say it?

We don't know how Mary Magdalene reacted when the disciples dismissed her. We don't even know for sure what happened in her life after she delivered this message. Tradition has her either traveling with the disciple John (or with Jesus's mom, depending on the source) to Ephesus to preach the gospel, or relocating to Provence, France, with Lazarus and his sisters Mary and Martha and evangelizing. Wouldn't it be cool if it was France? Because then both Joan of Arc and Mary

Magdalene landed in the same place. Either way, it is believed Mary Magdalene spent the rest of her life telling as many people as she could about Jesus and His redeeming love. What is God asking you to say?

To tell your family you're not going to watch that show because you wouldn't feel comfortable watching it if Jesus were in the room.

To start praying out loud each night with your roommate or spouse.

To suggest to that friend or coworker that they read a Christian book you believe God has nudged you to pass on to them.

To say you're sorry.

To tell the person who repeatedly hurts you that you're setting boundaries and distancing yourself from their toxic behavior.

To say no to the person, place, commitment, or thing that isn't good for you or would overextend you.

To tell someone you love that they need help.

To start a Bible study in your workplace and speak the truth over your coworkers.

Maybe speaking the words Jesus put in your heart makes you nervous. Maybe someone will disagree or dismiss or argue with you or try to make you feel small. Maybe they'll say no or laugh or try to talk you out of it. Or maybe they'll think it's a great idea, be so thrilled to know, feel relieved, be grateful, ask how they can help. I don't know how it will go down, but I do know if Jesus calls you to say it, you can. He'll empower you.

It's not about the outcome.

It's about the obedience.

Jesus never told Mary Magdalene, "Go and tell the disciples and they'll all be so excited they'll throw a party." Jesus just told her to go and tell them what she'd seen. Mary Magdalene did exactly that.

Was it to prepare the disciples' hearts for when Jesus appeared to them? Was it to convince the disciples once and for all that the impossible was possible with Jesus? Was it to grow Mary Magdalene's dependence on Jesus? Perhaps it was for all these reasons.

But as with most of our walks with Jesus, He'll ask us to say things that don't make sense to the rest of the world—that sometimes don't even make sense to us. Things people will question or dismiss. But

Jesus will have purpose in those words. We can bravely and obediently say what Jesus asks us to say, not worried about how people will react or respond, because we'll be serving our mighty and loving Lord. Like Joan of Arc and Mary Magdalene, we can go and tell.

Go and Tell Them

Jesus said, ". . . Go instead to my brothers and tell them, 'I am ascending to my Father and your Father, to my God and your God.'" (John 20:17)

- Is there something you've felt God nudging you to say? Or is there a group you've felt God nudging you to speak to? What's holding you back?
- Whether you've felt God asking you to go and tell someone something or not, there are always things He hopes we'll say. Spend five minutes asking Jesus to empower you to speak what He wants, when He wants, to who He wants. Ask Him for specific words and opportunities.

29

Do Life Together
Priscilla

Coffees from Kofenya in hand—a nonfat caramel latte for Brett and a mocha with macadamia milk for me—we strolled down the brick-lined street of our uptown and through the picturesque gates marking the entrance to the college campus where my husband works.

Weekend mornings in Oxford are typically quiet, but on this humid Sunday before church, music boomed from the academic quad. As we walked down Slant Walk, the path that cuts diagonally between the redbrick buildings and grassy patches, we were bombarded with posters, giant cutouts of Greek letters, and chattering college students. Mega Fair, which takes place near the beginning of each school year and showcases all the student organizations, was in full swing. There were tables encouraging students to sign up for everything from Best Buddies to the botany club to broomball (a sport similar to ice hockey but without skates). Remember Mike Wazowski passing tables for the improv club and art club in *Monsters University*? It's the same. But without monsters.

"I wonder if my L.I.F.E. group has a table?" Brett asked. "I hope they have a table . . ."

L.I.F.E. stands for Leading the Integration of Faith and Entrepreneurship. The club is part of the L.I.F.E. initiative Brett runs. L.I.F.E.

also includes research, academic conferences, and a class that teaches college students how integrating faith into their careers is a game changer. The club is a fairly new student organization that's just getting going. As we wove through college students in shorts and sneakers, we eventually found two L.I.F.E. members manning a table—empty except for a small stack of flyers. It was sandwiched between two other academic clubs with displays, photo boards, and snacks on their tables. We chatted with Justin and Sophia for a minute, then Brett said, "You guys could really use a sign. I have one at home. I could go get it." Brett looked at me as if to ask, "Is that okay?"

I nodded. "Sure, we could be back in ten minutes."

We walked back to where we'd parked, drove home, grabbed the sign, and returned. En route we brainstormed ways the students could spread the word about L.I.F.E., partner with other faith-based student organizations, improve their social media, and how we wished they'd put together any kind of display for their table. Brett even came up with a clever T-shirt design.

When we returned, we set up the sign, and Brett shared some of our ideas. All jazzed by the possibilities, he and Justin went off to introduce themselves to the students of other campus organizations while Sophia and I held down the fort, explaining what L.I.F.E. was to anyone who stopped and inviting them to the kickoff event the next day.

There was a buzz in the air—all these young people sharing things that excited them with wide-eyed freshmen eager to plug into university life. Some tables handed out bottles of water or candy or cupcakes. One had a giant moose mascot. The guitar club was playing acoustic music. A science club was performing some sort of experiment with goggles and smoke.

When Brett and Justin returned, I could sense Brett's adrenaline coursing. We strolled back to our car, and Brett said, "I'm sorry." He grabbed my hand and squeezed it. "So much for our walk. But thank you. I think it really helped them gain momentum and see how they could work with others." He unlocked the car. "These kids just didn't know where to start."

The interruption of our morning walk hadn't bothered me one bit.

I slid in the passenger seat. "It was great. Really. I have a lot of thoughts right now," I warned Brett before I rattled them off, because I can get going when I'm excited. "First, how cool that God put us here this morning. That we were walking along and literally stumbled into Mega Fair. And second, that we totally had time to go back home and get the sign and spend time with those students. That's not always the case. I feel like God really wanted us here and made it all happen." I took a sip of my coffee, warm and frothy. "Also, it felt so good to be able to help you, you know, for me to be able to participate in some of the awesome work you do. It's such a special part of living in a college town, of our marriage."

I love that the example of marriage in the New Testament reflects the kind of marriage God always had in mind, one where the couple works side by side for the betterment of God's kingdom—like the marriage of Priscilla. Or should I say, Priscilla and Aquila, because Priscilla is never mentioned in the Bible by herself. It is *always* Priscilla *and* Aquila (Acts 18:2, 18–19, 26; Romans 16:3; 1 Corinthians 16:19; 2 Timothy 4:19).

Together Priscilla and Aquila left Rome when the Jews were deported. They moved to Corinth together, where they ran their tent-making business. Priscilla and Aquila invited the apostle Paul, who was also a tentmaker, into their business and into their home. In sync with each other, Priscilla and Aquila left their home in Corinth and sailed with Paul to Ephesus, helping plant the church there. Many scholars believe Priscilla and Aquila financed this trip for Paul.[1] Together Priscilla and Aquila gracefully pulled Apollos aside when he was passionately but incorrectly preaching about Jesus. Together, in their home, they informed Apollos of the fullness of the good news of Jesus, equipping Apollos to later be a great preacher (Acts 18:28).

Their relationship sets a beautiful example, not just for couples but for how we can stand with someone we adore and work together to bravely further God's kingdom. For the singles reading this book, do you have a friendship like this? One where you build God's kingdom together side by side? Do you encourage your married friends to work in tandem for the glory of God?

We can stand with someone we adore and work together to bravely further God's kingdom.

For the married readers, is this what your marriage looks like? Do you help your spouse with their work? Do you invite people into your home? Are you willing to move together if God asks you to? Do you make joint decisions on your finances? United, do you help others discover the truth of Christ's love?

In his book *Loveology*, John Mark Comer writes, "All healthy marriages are built around a calling. Marriage . . . exists for friendship, yes [and sexuality and family], but also to partner with God for the remaking of shalom."[2]

This is beautiful. And true. And for the record, I believe deep friendships can do the same—partner with God for the remaking of shalom: the fullness, completeness, welfare, health, and peace of the earth and the relationships in it.[3]

Dang. Priscilla and Aquila had this figured out. They partnered with God so humans could flourish in His love, so they could hear about, understand, and share the love of Christ. They worked together to earn an income that allowed them to do this, and that also enabled them to support others in kingdom work. Priscilla and Aquila went where God called them and started a church in their home.

I love this! Because, yes, Brett is my very best friend on the planet. We adore our family. And intimacy is a beautiful thing God created for a husband and wife to connect and give of themselves to one another. But also, we support each other with our vocations. With the work God has called us specifically to do. And it is a rich, fulfilling aspect of our marriage.

This can look like fetching a sign for Mega Fair, brainstorming for L.I.F.E., or my speaking to Brett's class. It could look like grilling out for dinner—me marinating the fish, slicing the juicy tomatoes from the farmers' market, husking and boiling the corn, while Brett stands over the flames of the hot grill and then washes the dishes afterward. Together we feed our family. Which I promise is kingdom work. It could mean Brett carrying boxes of books out to the car for me before a speaking event or us praying over proposals we've sent out or for safety for our travel. This includes standing up at church together and lighting an Advent candle, sharing each other's social media posts about our kingdom work, raking heaps of leaves on crisp fall Saturdays to create shalom in our home, and praying for our kids together.

If our children approach me with tricky questions—Can they stay out past their curfew? Go on a certain trip? Drop a class?—I try to respond with, "Thank you for coming to me and explaining the situation. Let me talk with Dad about it and I'll let you know tomorrow."

Brett does the same.

It's all kingdom work, an attempt to bravely restore a little bit of our world, our family, our home more to its original Eden-like state than when we found it.

Do we do everything together? Nope. We're not supposed to. I spend hours alone in my writing nook, stringing sentences together. Most of Brett's work at the university is done on campus or with his colleagues. I love to bake and read novels. Brett does not. Brett plays golf and cheers on the Bengals. I don't swing a club and can't name four professional football players. I'm part of a great group of women from our church who study the Bible together. Brett has an amazing small group of Christian entrepreneurs he meets with weekly for prayer and support.

But also, moments like Mega Fair pop up, and then I get to be a coworker in Christ with my husband, and it's different from the work we do separately. There's an extra energy to it, a privilege that we get to further God's kingdom together.

Our friends Shena and Shawn host and lead a couples' Bible study. For six consecutive Fridays each spring, they prepare dinner for half a dozen young couples. They hire a babysitter to watch everyone's littles while the grown-ups dive into what the Bible says about marriage. Shena and Shawn also helped move their in-laws and cared for nieces and nephews together when there was a family emergency. They are creating spaces for God and His people to walk freely together.

My friend Alli's husband is an attorney who set up a nonprofit for her to extend her ministry beyond her church. He regularly reviews contracts and intellectual property agreements as she writes and speaks. My friend Amy's husband runs a production company. When she needs a video filmed for her website or to promote her latest book, he films and edits it for her. They're building the kingdom together.

Again, kingdom-building relationships aren't reserved for marriage. A couple of college girls I know started their own business selling T-shirts with wonderful declarations of who we are in Christ printed across the front. My mom and her girlfriends stuff Easter baskets with goodies for underprivileged kids in their community each year. Alli, Amy, and I created a Bible study together, review each other's books, are on each other's podcasts, and pray for each other. There are all kinds of ways to partner to bravely bring shalom to earth.

God wants this to be an integral part of our relationships.

> The LORD God said, "It is not good for the man to be alone. I will make a helper suitable for him." . . .
> But for Adam no suitable helper was found. So the LORD God caused the man to fall into a deep sleep; and while he was sleeping, he took one of the man's ribs and then closed up the place with flesh. Then the LORD God made a woman from the rib he had taken out of the man, and he brought her to the man.
> The man said,
>
> > "This is now bone of my bones
> > and flesh of my flesh;
> > she shall be called 'woman,'
> > for she was taken out of man."
>
> That is why a man leaves his father and mother and is united to his wife, and they become one flesh. (Genesis 2:18, 20–24)

One flesh. Working together for God. To help each other in this work. This was always God's plan.

Do Brett and I do this perfectly?

Of course not.

Are there days when I'm so focused on what I'm doing that I get selfish and want more time to do "my" things and even get annoyed when he asks for help with something? Yup. Are there days when I could really use a hand, and Brett has back-to-back meetings that get him home late, and we both end up feeling frazzled and like we're fighting uphill battles alone? Uh huh.

But overall, we do this life together. We work together—in our careers but also to maintain our household, raise our children, support worthy causes, and host people in our home.

God knew from the beginning that Priscilla and Aquila would need each other to bravely flee in exile, move again, start a business, host a traveling missionary, correct incorrect teaching, and plant a church. It would have been too much for either of them to do alone. It wouldn't have been as complete without both of their insights, both of their personalities, both of their understandings. Our mighty God brought Priscilla and Aquila together to enable them to find strength and courage in each other so they could do all these things and do them well.

Was one of them more organized than the other? Was one of them more adventurous? Was Priscilla great at doing the accounting for the business and Aquila better at stitching the fabric for tents? We don't know, but we do know that God joined them together to help one another, that this is one of the reasons why God created marriage in the first place.

There is so much kingdom work to be done. The old saying "two heads are better than one" rings true. God empowers us to create more shalom by putting special people in our lives. This holds true for marriage but also for godly friendships. Because with shared skill sets, insights, passions, abilities, time, and energy and the ways our mighty God emboldens us, we can create some more peace on earth and remind each other of the God who created us in the first place.

Do Life Together

The LORD God said, "It is not good for the man to be alone. I will make a helper suitable for him." (Genesis 2:18)

- If you're married, do you assist your spouse in their calling like Priscilla and Aquila did?
- If you're single, do you have a close friend that you work together with to bring shalom to earth?
- Make a list of two things you'd like to do this week for the kingdom. How can you invite your spouse or a valued friend into that work?
- Ask your spouse or friend how you could work with them this week to advance human flourishing and others' ability to walk with God.

30

Use Your Gifts

Lydia

My friend Juiquetta tells the story of how she had to shave one hundred balloons with a straight-edge razor without popping a single one to get her barber's license. She said the barber school figured if you could keep one hundred balloons safe, you could shave someone's face without cutting it. Juiquetta, who also goes by the nickname Kiki the Barber, owns a local barber shop and does a whole lot more than cut hair.

"Hold your head up," she'll instruct customers as she trims around their ears, "You are a part of a royal family." A few minutes later she insists over the hum of her electric shears, "Sit up. You're a son of the King."

Slumped-over middle schoolers sit up straighter; exhausted fire-fighters exhale. Dads, professors, construction workers, and lawyers seem to grow a few inches taller in her swiveling seat as they consider that they are royalty. Juiquetta talks openly about her faith with her customers, even reading Scripture and praying with those who are intrigued by the God and King she talks about. Kiki uses the gifts God gave her—scissors, a chair, an artist's eye—and does as Jesus instructs us.

You are the light of the world. A town built on a hill cannot be hidden. Neither do people light a lamp and put it under a bowl. Instead they put it on its stand, and it gives light to everyone in the house. In the same way, let your light shine before others, that they may see your good deeds and glorify your Father in heaven. (Matthew 5:14–16)

Juiquetta is a bright light, shining Christ's love to everyone who walks into her shop.

So is my friend Beth, who teaches a creativity class at the local university. Her job is to help students think outside the box, help them see in color what they've only been seeing in black and white. Through her interaction with college students, Beth has grown a community of young women she encourages, empowers, and inspires. Using Christian principles, Beth reminds these college girls of their value and challenges them to be brave, pursue their dreams, and not let anything stop them. At the same time, Beth equips these young ladies not just with aspirations but tangible tools of the trade to enable them to build brands, start companies, launch websites.

God made Beth creative, intelligent, and a gifted teacher. He also put her in the classroom. Beth's work at a public university is like a prism, taking Christ's light, shining it through herself, and letting those beams of the rainbow spread outward in an immeasurable ripple effect. Because Beth builds into these young women, they go on to do wonderful work that inspires others.

Juiquetta and Beth are doing "secular" work, meaning they don't work for a church or a ministry. But I promise these women are doing the work of the Father, acting as the hands and feet of Jesus, shining Christ's light right where they are, and using the gifts God gave them.

You can do this too.

You are the light of the world.

Ready to shine?

You don't have to have all the pieces figured out or a ton of background knowledge. God will empower you to shine His light. He will charge you up and make you bright. You just need to step onto the hill where He's called you, use the gifts He's already given you, and shine and radiate His love.

God empowered a woman named Lydia who was just doing her own thing. He lit a flame inside her and she shined it so brightly.

> On the Sabbath we [Paul, Silas, and Luke] went outside the city gate to the river, where we expected to find a place of prayer. We sat down and began to speak to the women who had gathered there. One of those listening was a woman from the city of Thyatira named Lydia, a dealer in purple cloth. She was a worshiper of God. The Lord opened her heart to respond to Paul's message. When she and the members of her household were baptized, she invited us to her home. "If you consider me a believer in the Lord," she said, "come and stay at my house." (Acts 16:13–15)

Lydia went to the river outside the gate for weekly prayer meetings. She was seeking God and His will. While in the thriving city of Philippi, Paul, Luke, and Silas stopped by this gathering to tell the people worshiping God about Jesus. Lydia, a successful businesswoman, heard the good news that Jesus nailed our sins to the cross, rose from the dead, and that she, along with all God's children (that's you and me), could be in a close, loving relationship with Jesus forevermore.

Lydia was so thrilled by this revelation that she got baptized as a public declaration of her faith. As a well-known member of a textile guild and an influencer in her community, people took note of what Lydia did. When she shared about Jesus's open invitation for everyone to join God's kingdom, the entire household she managed also got baptized.

Later, when Paul and Silas were put in jail and then released, their first stop was Lydia's. When they arrived, Lydia's home was filled with believers (Acts 16:40). Her household is where these traveling missionaries felt safe and where they wanted to share about the earthquake God created that opened the doors of the prison, broke the chains of every prisoner, and convinced the jailer and everyone in his household that Jesus was Lord.

Lydia didn't have formal training in theology, a job at a synagogue, or any previous knowledge about Jesus. But those weren't hindrances to Lydia, because our mighty God gave her the resources she needed and made her brave enough to use them. God gifted Lydia a lucrative business and the savvy that enabled her to grow and maintain that business, which enabled her to afford a large home where she could house lots of people and had room to host guests, like Paul and Silas. Lydia could also start a house church in her spacious home. God gave Lydia a belief in Him and a heart that sought Him. Lydia exemplifies how when we seek God, He can and will use the gifts He's given us in our existing spheres of life to add vibrancy to the world.

In Paul's opening of his letter to the Philippians, he was joyful about the church Lydia was leading and confident in the good work being done there.

> I thank my God every time I remember you. In all my prayers for all of you, I always pray with joy because of your partnership in the gospel from the first day until now, being confident of this, that he who began a good work in you will carry it on to completion until the day of Christ Jesus. (1:3–6)

God gifted Lydia with everything she needed to do this good work, to carry it out to completion. God gifted my friend Juiquetta to cut hair, but also to build up her clients' self-esteem. God set up Beth with teaching skills and a job at our local university where she daily interacts with students from around the globe, inspiring them to use the gifts God has given them.

The Message's translation of Jesus's teaching us to shine our lights is worded like this: "Here's another way to put it: You're here to be light, bringing out the God-colors in the world" (Matthew 5:14 MSG).

God-colors? I'm guessing they're magnificent, more vibrant than the bright red of a strawberry or the vivid yellow of a goldfinch. God-colors are breathtaking. Bringing out those in our world? It's noble work.

When we seek God, He can and
will use the gifts He's given us in
our existing spheres of life to
add vibrancy to the world.

I think of Lydia, who is known as "a dealer in purple cloth." Purple was a rare color. The plants that made purple dye were hard to come by, expensive. Lydia made this bright cloth, adding splashes of a rarely seen color into the world, opening the eyes of those around her to possibilities they'd never dreamed of before. Yes, possibilities of purples, unseen, seemingly literal God-colors. But also of metaphorical God-colors—God's perfect, unfathomable love.

God also empowers you and me to bring out the God-colors of the world. Yes, us. Right where we are. He gifts us everything we need and makes us brave enough to use those gifts.

I recently had a friend who didn't feel that was possible. She told me, "I'm floundering with my purpose."

That's easy to feel when you're in between things or you're working a job you don't love or your marriage feels rocky or you're in a new town and don't know anyone or you're getting part-time hours when you want full-time or the weight of depression feels heavy. But God loves you and sees you everywhere you go and in every situation you're in. God wants you to be confident that not only did He start a good work in you by planting ideas, sprinkling in talents, and opening doors, but He will also do something powerful with all those ideas and gifts. He won't let that spark He lit inside you sit stagnant. Jesus will use it to light up the world.

So where does God have you today? Volunteering as the art mom or cafeteria helper at your kids' school? You can shine Christ's light there to the students and staff. Cleaning people's homes to make some extra cash? You can bless those people with kind words and understanding. Leading a conference, heading up a team, writing songs, treating patients, working shifts at an ice cream shop? You have gifts from God and access to people with struggles who could use a pep talk, a prayer, or a positive voice in their lives. People who need a reminder that God loves them, a word of encouragement, maybe even a hug. People who feel stark or gray whom you have the ability to help see the God-colors within and around them.

Yes, if you're passionate in learning more about Jesus you can enroll in seminary (I have two girlfriends currently in seminary and I'm so proud of them), plant your own church like Lydia did, or start a Christian blog, YouTube channel, or T-shirt company. Those are all super ways to shine Christ's light. But you can also walk dogs or set up a stand at the local farmers' market selling the earrings you make or the vegetables you grow using your gifts to create more beauty in God's world. You can do all the hard math for your company's budgeting and taxes and forecasts or teach a spin class or drive your kids to and from practice and spread the good news of Jesus's love in your office, gym, or car. You can be the one who is kind and positive, the one who listens well, the one who has just the skill or connection to make all the difference whether you're in the boardroom, the back room, or the locker room.

So what gifts has God given you? What are you good at? What resources do you have? What stage of life are you in? Where does God have you in this season? The barber shop, classroom, riverbank?

Don't worry about what you'll say or how to use your gifts. Our mighty God is with you whether you're in the chair or cutting the hair, teaching or taking the class. God has given you the gifts you need and the bravery and ability to use them. And He's asking you, like Lydia, Kiki, and Beth, to stand up and bring out the God-colors of this world.

Use Your Gifts

Here's another way to put it: You're here to be light, bringing out the God-colors in the world. (Matthew 5:14 MSG)

- Let's do a little self-assessment.

    Where do you go on a regular basis?

    Who do you encounter there?

    What are some skills or talents God has given you? Are you a good listener, great at strategizing, creative, a master of details, or do you have a way with children?

    What are some resources God has given you? Do you have a car that could provide transportation, a video camera, a home where you can host others, a lawn mower, toys your kids have outgrown, baking pans?

- Brainstorm two ways you can use the gifts God has given you to shine Christ's light to someone you'll encounter in the next week. Be inspired by Lydia and how she took what she had and used it to grow God's kingdom.

    Take time to journal how those encounters went.

You Are Brave and Can Do Mighty Things

The bravery to live a life worth living doesn't come from obeying all the rules or following five easy steps. We won't thrive by knowing all the answers, reading a self-help book, winning the race, or redecorating our house. We get our power, our joy, our purpose, our self-worth, and the bravery to live it all out directly from Jesus. We don't have to strive or prove our value in order to be with Him or to access this power. The Holy Spirit lives in us (1 Corinthians 6:19). He is with us everywhere we go and in everything we do.

The women of the Bible experienced this firsthand. Most of them encountered God in the everyday—on the streets or in their homes, making a meal, doing their work, or at their very worst, loneliest, or most frightened. Through their stories, we've seen that God can be encountered while running away from one's master, lost in the desert, or while filling a bucket of water, alone, in the despised town of Samaria. God's abundance can be experienced when the food or resources or time seem to have run out. Christ's protection and compassion can be felt even when we're caught in sin, thrown on the street, or accused. While we're alone in our bedrooms, feeling like life is over, Jesus takes our hand and invites us to "get up" so we can step into more and more life. Even when we're grieving or confused, Jesus can still embolden us to go and share the good news of His love.

Jesus wants us to talk to Him. He longs to hear all our hopes and dreams and worries and fears and is so grateful when we pray. Jesus loves it when we attend church, learn more about Him, worship Him, and hang out with other believers. Jesus adores it when we read the Bible to dive into His living Word and His loving promises because when we do, it drowns out the lies of the world and reminds us of the truth of His grace.

But even when we're just doing our normal things, our day-to-day things—our commuting to work, cutting grilled cheese into triangles, wiping down counters, texting a friend, tying our gym shoes—He is there. Mighty Jesus is with you and me, giving us the courage and clarity to do things we could never do on our own, equipping and encouraging us to do amazing, miraculous things for our good and His glory.

Let's not overlook this. That the actual power of our mighty God is alive in each of us.

Today, no matter what we're facing or experiencing, we can be brave. Jesus will equip us to call out the lies, be the change, break bad cycles, say yes, rise up, use our gifts, and so much more.

You don't have to do any of these things by yourself, in your own strength, with your own resources. You were never meant to. But you can bravely do whatever God has set in front of you, infinitely more than you could ever ask, think, or imagine (Ephesians 3:20), because the Almighty has empowered you to do it.

Acknowledgments

Jesus, You make me brave. Thank You for empowering me to do more than I could ever hope, think, or imagine.

Brett, like God used Hosea to show Gomer what His love looks like, God uses you every day to show me what His beautiful love looks like. Thank you for loving me like that, for reminding me of who I am in Christ, for cheering me on, for making me braver than I thought I could ever be, and for helping me thrive. I love you more than you will ever know.

Maddie and Mallory (a.k.a. Two Sisters), do you have any idea how brave you make me? You remind me that I am enough, that I can use my voice and express my feelings. You give me confidence and joy and make me laugh. You encourage me to be the best version of myself. You inspire me on a daily basis with all the brave things you do. Thank you. I love you both for exactly who you are, always.

Max and Maguire, thank you for treating me and your sisters with honor and respect, for lifting us up and embracing our stories. Thank you for standing up for us and holding us tight and loving us well. You both are a blessing to the women of this world. I am so grateful I get to be your mom, and I love you so much.

Mom, you are a role model of what a brave woman looks like. You have braved so many storms and clung to Jesus and His love every step of the way. Thank you for shining your light so brightly so others can see the God-colors in the world. I aspire to be like you. I love you and am forever grateful for you.

Thank you to my incredible team of brave women at Kregel Publications. I'm so excited and blessed to be working with you all on this project. Specifically, Catherine DeVries, thank you for believing in this book and its message. Rachel Kirsch, thank you for coffee, swapping tales of our favorite women in the Bible, and overseeing this book from start to finish. Caryn Rivadeneira and Emily Irish, I'm grateful for your editorial skills and wisdom. You made this book shine. Lisa Grimenstein and Lindsay Danielson, thank you for dotting my i's and crossing my t's. Sarah Cross, thank you for listening to the heartbeat of this book and overseeing the marketing to share it with the world. Caroline Cahoon, thank you for the most gorgeous cover ever. I cried happy tears when I saw it. Because of each of your work and dedication, this book reminds us all to be brave and how our mighty God is on the move in our lives.

Bob Hostetler, thank you for being a champion of women in the church, and for this woman writer. I am grateful for your years of support and guidance as my agent.

Amy (a.k.a. Ruth), you give me the courage to keep writing and remind me of God's call on my life when I forget. You show me what brave looks like. Thank you for always being there and always encouraging and empowering me (and always being willing to eat chocolate or giggle with me too).

Shena, you are my favorite person to talk about the women of the Bible with. Thank you for being the friend who will listen to what Jesus is doing in my life or about my new running shoes or about fashion or family or books. You make me braver to dream the dreams God has put in my heart.

Tammy, you are beautifully brave and such a loyal, loving friend. I am grateful for years of friendship and seeking the Lord together.

Kristan, you make so many women, including me, braver by giving them the tools to lean into Jesus and His strength. Thank you for how you lead the women at Anthem House Church and for your authentic friendship.

Playlist

"We Say Yes," Housefires
"Don't Fight Alone," Jon Reddick
"You Make Me Brave," Bethel Music, Amanda Cook
"What I See," Elevation Worship, Chris Brown
"This Love," Housefires
"Came to My Rescue," Hillsong UNITED
"Fighting for Me," Riley Clemmons
"By Your Side," Tenth Avenue North
"Help Is on the Way," Amanda Cook
"Champion," Bethel Music, Dante Bowe
"Rescue," Lauren Daigle
"Fishes and Loaves," Josiah Queen
"Mighty One," Maverick City Music, Todd Dulaney
"The Heart of Worship," Matt Redman
"Good Good Father," Housefires, Chandler Moore
"40," U2
"Amazing Grace," Carrie Underwood
"Joyful," Dante Bowe
"Reason to Praise," Bethel Music, Cory Asbury, Naomi Raine
"Honey in the Rock," Brooke Ligertwood, Brandon Lake
"Defender," Jesus Culture, Katie Torwalt
"Raise a Hallelujah," Bethel Music, Jonathan David Helser, Melissa Helser

Notes

Introduction
1. C. S. Lewis, *The Lion, the Witch and the Wardrobe* (Harper-Collins, 1950; repr., Scholastic, 1995), 189. Citations refer to the Scholastic edition.

Chapter 2: Hold Out for Happily-Ever-After
1. Strong's Hebrew Lexicon (NIV), "H8283—śārâ," Blue Letter Bible, accessed November 19, 2024, www.blueletterbible.org/lexicon/h8283/niv/wlc/0-1.
2. Strong's Hebrew Lexicon (NIV), "H8297—śāray," Blue Letter Bible, accessed November 19, 2024, www.blueletterbible.org/lexicon/h8297/niv/wlc/0-1.

Chapter 3: Call for Help
1. "Statistics," National Sexual Violence Resource Center, accessed November 19, 2024, www.nsvrc.org/statistics.
2. If you've been sexually assaulted, the National Sexual Assault Hotline is available 24/7 at 1-800-656-4673 with someone safe who can help.

Chapter 4: Walk Through the Door
1. C. S. Lewis, *Prince Caspian* (HarperCollins, 1951; repr.,

Scholastic, 1995), 142, emphasis added. Citations refer to the Scholastic edition.

Chapter 6: Sing
1. Jonathan Helser in "Raise a Hallelujah (LIVE)—Jonathan and Melissa Helser | VICTORY," by Jake Stevens, Jonathan David Helser, Melissa Helser, and Molly Skaggs, Bethel Music, 2019, www.youtube.com/watch?v=awkO61T6i0k.

Chapter 7: Do the Crazy Thing
1. Henry H. Halley, *Halley's Bible Handbook* (Zondervan, 1962), 159.

Chapter 10: Forge Friendships
1. C. S. Lewis, *The Voyage of the Dawn Treader* (HarperCollins, 1952; repr., Scholastic, 1995), 187. Citations refer to the Scholastic edition.
2. "Tragedy Strikes the Family of Ruth and Naomi (Ruth 1:1–22)," Theology of Work Project, May 15, 2013, www.theologyofwork.org/old-testament/ruth-and-work/tragedy-strikes-the-family-of-ruth-and-naomi-ruth-11-22.

Chapter 11: Go from Bitter to Sweet
1. "Ruth and Naomi: Follow Their Path from Bethlehem to Moab on a Biblical Journey," Living Passages, accessed July 8, 2024, https://livingpassages.com/footsteps-ruth-and-naomi.
2. "My Hope Is Built on Nothing Less" by Edward Mote is in the public domain.

Chapter 16: Break the Cycle
1. John Mark Comer, *God Has a Name* (Zondervan, 2017), 248, emphasis added.
2. Sarah Epstein, "If My Parents Are Divorced, Is My Marriage Doomed to Fail?," *Psychology Today*, February 5, 2019, www.psychologytoday.com/us/blog/between-the-generations/201902/if-my-parents-are-divorced-is-my-marriage-doomed-fail.

Chapter 17: Keep Them Safe
1. Miep Gies, *Anne Frank Magazine*, 1998, quoted in "Miep Gies," Anne Frank House, accessed July 8, 2024, www.annefrank.org /en/anne-frank/main-characters/miep-gies.
2. Tyler Piccotti, "Harriet Tubman," Biography.com, updated December 11, 2023, www.biography.com/activist/harriet-tubman.
3. Piccotti, "Harriet Tubman."

Chapter 18: Answer Their Questions
1. This story is also recorded in 2 Kings 22.

Chapter 19: Step into Freedom
1. Amy Novotney, "7 in 10 Human Trafficking Victims Are Women and Girls. What Are the Psychological Effects?," American Psychological Association, April 24, 2023, www.apa.org/topics /women-girls/trafficking-women-girls.
2. Francine Rivers, *Redeeming Love* (Multnomah, 1997), 35.
3. David C. Bricker and Jeffrey E. Young, "A Client's Guide to Schema Therapy," Cognitive Therapy Center, 2012, https:// cognitivebehaviortherapycenter.com/schema-therapy-califor nia/client-guide-schema-therapy/.
4. Aruna Project, "Priya's Story," *Aruna* (blog), November 7, 2021, https://arunaproject.com/blogs/aruna-blog/priya-s-story.

Chapter 20: Say Yes
1. Strong's Hebrew Lexicon (NIV), "G1298—diatarassō," Blue Letter Bible, accessed November 19, 2024, www.blueletterbible .org/lexicon/g1298/niv/mgnt/0-1.

Chapter 21: Jump for Joy
1. Nicole Zasowski, in an Instagram post by Laura L. Smith (@laura smithauthor), "How do you find wonderful no matter what your current circumstances are? Join me while I chat with @nicole zasowski for some inspiration," Instagram Live recording, July 17, 2023, https://www.instagram.com/p/Cu0KfQjNd5w.

2. Nicole Zasowski (@nicolezasowski), "Here you go! The practice that helps us tolerate the vulnerability of joy! If you haven't read yesterday's post, you might like to take a look at that first 😊," Instagram Reel, July 20, 2023, https://www.instagram.com/p/Cu7TjbOA_Dm.

Chapter 22: Be Patient
1. "Reconstruction Continues at the Cathedral of Notre Dame 4 Years After Fire," *60 Minutes*, August 27, 2023, CBS News, www.cbsnews.com/video/notre-dame-cathedral-restoration-60-minutes-video-2023-08-27.

Chapter 24: Quench Your Thirst
1. Henri Nouwen, "Who Are We? Henri Nouwen on Our Christian Identity," podcast-style audio course, Learn25, 2017, MP3 audio.
2. Nouwen, "Who Are We?"

Chapter 28: Go and Tell Them
1. The disciple John was at the crucifixion, but we have no record of the other male disciples being there.

Chapter 29: Do Life Together
1. John R. W. Stott, *The Spirit, the Church, and the World* (InterVarsity, 1990), 300.
2. John Mark Comer, *Loveology: God. Love. Marriage. Sex. And the Never-Ending Story of Male and Female* (Zondervan, 2013), 60.
3. Strong's Hebrew Lexicon (NIV), "H7965—šālôm," Blue Letter Bible, accessed November 19, 2024, www.blueletterbible.org/lexicon/h7965/kjv/wlc/0-1.

About the Author

 Laura L. Smith is the author of several books, including *The Urgency of Slowing Down* and *Holy Care for the Whole Self.* She is also a podcaster and frequent speaker at Christian events around the country. She lives in Oxford, Ohio, with her husband and the youngest of their four young adult kids. Learn more at laurasmithauthor.com.